Third Ways

Culture of Enterprise series

_____

Third Ways

How Bulgarian Greens,
Swedish Housewives, and Beer-Swilling
Englishmen Created
Family-Centered Economies—
and Why They Disappeared

Allan C. Carlson

Wilmington, Delaware

The Culture of Enterprise series is supported by a grant from the John Templeton Foundation. The Intercollegiate Studies institute gratefully acknowledges this support.

Carlson, Allan C.

Third ways: how Bulgarian greens, Swedish housewives, and beerswilling Englishmen created family-centered economies—and why they disappeared / Allan C. Carlson.—1st ed.—Wilmington, Del.: ISI Books, 2007.

p. ; cm.
(Culture of enterprise)

ISBN: 978-1-933859-40-8
Includes bibliographical references and index.

1. Economics—Sociological aspects. 2. Family—Economic aspects. 3. Family-owned business enterprises. 4. Family farms—Economic aspects. I. Title. II. Series.

HM548 .C37   2007 2007933850
306.3/01—dc22   0710

Published in the United States by:
ISI Books
Intercollegiate Studies Institute
Post Office Box 4431
Wilmington, DE 19807-0431
wwww.isibooks.org

Manufactured in the United States of America

TO THE MEMORY OF
EDWIN AND DOROTHY BELL BELIN

Contents

Preface

The twentieth century witnessed a great contest between rival social, economic, and political systems: liberal capitalism versus communism. From the Bolshevik Revolution of 1917 to the disintegration of the Soviet Union in 1991, this conflict was especially intense. Capitalism's elevation of the individual, private property, and free markets contrasted with communism's emphasis on collective identity, state ownership of property, and central planning. Circumstances pushed individuals, and nations, to declare for one side or the other, especially during the Cold War era of 1946–91.

However, many balked at making this stark choice. During the 1920s and 1930s, some were lured by the siren songs of fascism and national socialism. The former promised, although never really delivered, an economy resting on a renewal of the medieval guilds. The latter subordinated the economy, as all else, to the quest for racial empire. Through a strange sequence of events, the capitalist and Communist nations stumbled into shaky alliance during 1941–45 to battle and eventually crush these pretenders.

This volume examines a very different search among some Europeans and North Americans for a Third Way, a form of social and economic organization that in important respects would be neither capitalist nor Communist. Unlike the fascists and Nazis, these searchers were committed to the ideals of democracy—especially economic democracy—and pluralism. Unlike liberal capitalists, they refused to treat human labor and relationships as commodities. They also sought to protect and renew the "natural" communities of family, village, neighborhood, and parish. Unlike Communists, these searchers defended private property in land and capital goods and underscored the dignity and rights of individuals and families. Unlike both liberal capitalists and Communists, they treasured rural culture, family-scale farming, gender complementarity, and the vital household economy.

All the same, this quest for a Third Way never jelled into one course of united action. Instead, it would effervesce in different places and times. Sometimes it appeared as formal theory, rich in intellectual content. Other times, it arose out of communities of interest or mass organization, expressing a common will and platform. Still other times, it became visible through practical political action. On all these occasions, the search bore fruit in events of brilliance and excitement, sometimes reaching fruition, only to fade again in the face of the two main contestants, capitalism and communism, or their curious joint offspring, the Servile State.

This book examines, sequentially, seven distinct episodes in this ill-fated search for a Third Way. The first chapter takes a fresh look at Distributism, the economic project advanced by English authors Hilaire Belloc and G. K. Chesterton that sought broad property ownership, small-scale production, and agrarian reform. It revises our understanding of this movement by outlining the real legacy of this program and the crucial contemporary import of Belloc's concept of the Servile State. Chapter 2 looks at a less theoretical, equally populist strategy to shelter marriages, homes, and children from the industrial principle: the family wage regime, which bent market signals and the structure of the labor force to reinforce family autonomy. It emphasizes the real results achieved, and the profound social costs when the system disintegrated.

Chapter 3 focuses on Alexander Chayanov, a Russian agricultural economist who fashioned a complex analysis of the "natural family economy" and a powerful argument for preservation of the peasant mode of production in Russia. This analysis also gives attention to Chayanov's delightful novella, *The Land of Peasant Utopia*. The fourth chapter explores the goals and fates of peasant political parties that came to power in Bulgaria, Romania, and Poland after World War I. It sees real promise behind this "Green Rising" as a practical interwar alternative to fascism, finance capitalism, and communism, as well as the tragedy behind its failure.

The fifth chapter examines a curious phenomenon: the emergence of "socialist housewives" in Sweden as a genuine political and economic force that attempted to keep both collectivism and individualism out of working-class homes. This examination reveals that a distinctive ideology and successful political mobilization characterized this largely forgotten and poorly understood movement. Chapter 6 returns to the theoretical plane, looking at the theories of economic historian Karl Polanyi, particularly his concepts of the "economy without markets," the "great transformation," and "the always embedded market economy." This analysis underscores Polanyi's unease over *homo economicus* and other core liberal economic doctrines in addition to his defense of families, small property, and agrarian life.

The seventh chapter looks to the emergence of Christian Democracy as a distinctive economic program focused on social justice and the well- being of families and other organic communities. It emphasizes the influence of economist Wilhelm Röpke and his concept of *homo religiosus* as the foundation of the moral economy. A concluding chapter draws the lessons from these seven episodes by asking several questions: Why did they all fail in the end? Was liberal capitalism the ultimate victor? Or did some other ideological construct actually win out?

All of these Third Way episodes shared a common grounding in true democracy, respect for the human person, allegiance to the natural communities of family and village, private property, reverence toward traditional ways, and family-scale economies. The usual result, however, was failure—sometimes deeply trag- ic in nature and scope. Looming over the whole story is wistful regret over lost opportunities, ones that might have spared tens of millions of lives and forestalled the blights of fascism, Stalin- ism, socialism, and the peculiar Servile State. And yet, out of this journey into largely forgotten history, one might also draw fresh hope for human possibilities and prospects in this our new century and millennium.

I owe thanks to a number of organizations and individuals for their help and encouragement. A research grant from the Ear- hart Foundation of Ann Arbor, Michigan, provided opportuni- ties to visit several specialized archives and the time to draft the manuscript. My colleagues at The Howard Center for Family, Religion & Society—notably Bryce Christensen, Heidi Gee, John Howard, Lawrence Jacobs, and George Marlin—lent spe- cial forms of help and support. Bill Kauffman, a gifted writer and able editor, gave detailed and valued editorial advice. The team at the Intercollegiate Studies Institute associated with this project—especially Jeremy Beer, Richard Brake, and Mark Henrie—made the project possible and shaped its contents for the better. Others who encouraged it in varied ways in- cluded Stellan Andersson, Arne Bengtsson, Father Ian Boyd, Alan Crippen II, Yvonne Hirdman, Paul Mero, and Douglas

Minson. Finally, I thank the principals of the John Templeton Foundation for understanding that a truly competitive and humane economy must rest within a healthy culture and for their support of this special book series.

1

"ChesterBelloc" and the
Fairy Tale of Distributism

Biographers and historians have not been kind to Distributism, the economic program, jointly advanced by Hilaire Belloc and G. K. Chesterton, that focused on bringing about agrarian reform, encouraging small-scale production, and expanding the ownership of private property. Michael Mason, for example, blasts the very concept of "Chesterbelloc," calling this shorthand label for Distributism—as invented by George Bernard Shaw—a "fabulous beast" that existed only in Shaw's head. Belloc was a man of action, while his "unwilling partner" Chesterton was "content to live in the imagination." The differences between the two "were greater than the commonly held virtues of Catholicism, food, drink, conversation and laughter"; Distributism itself was fantastical.[1]

Canadian author Michael Coren is more scathing in his judgments. He labels Distributist arguments "ludicrous," "arrogant," and "naïve rather than unpleasant, relying on wishful thinking and ignorance of world affairs." He notes the tendency "for reactionary views to creep" into Distributist analysis, so that "the nasty flavour of economic fascism . . . is strong indeed." Overall, Distributism "smacks of one thing: extremism."[2]

Even sympathetic writers reach negative conclusions. Examining the "classical period of Distributism" (1926–36), *Chesterton Review* editor Ian Boyd expresses surprise over "how little" this "large mass of material . . . tells one about the details of the programme." There is "an extraordinarily limited amount of agreement" on common policy.[3] Ronald Knox underscores the chaos of Distributist writing: "it is not exactly a doctrine, or a philosophy, it is simply Chesterton's reaction to life."[4] Joseph Pearce sees Belloc's rejection of both capitalism and communism as tempting him into the "treacherous waters" of proto-fascism.[5] A. N. Wilson finds the aims and principles of Distributism to be "childishly simple."[6] Biographer Dudley Barker concludes that Chesterton propagated a theory "without any conception of the practice":

> He had no idea of how a farmer farmed (or how his own gardener grew vegetables); he had probably never been inside a modern factory and he had no knowledge of machinery or business practices—he certainly could not have run a confectionary shop successfully for a day.[7]

Still others fault Distributism for its frivolity and its failure to generate political consequences. Chesterton biographer Margaret Canovan focuses on the movement's "lack of popular support."[8] The youthful Distributist Brocard Sewell accuses the program of having been "too alien" ever to catch on. Within the Distributist League, "the lack of funds was chronic," the members were "mostly poor," women were absent (for "Distributism was always essentially a man's movement . . . another of its limitations and weaknesses"), and most of the local branches were frail, degenerating into mere debating societies.[9] Meanwhile, the movement's magazine carried approving reports "of bizarre attempts by League members to set up primitive and self-sufficient rural settlements."[10]

Such judgments multiply. The Distributist project "was a sure flop politically,"[11] attracting an increasingly weird collection of "cranks of various hues."[12] Canovan calls the Distributist League "a sorry spectacle."[13] Coren is disdainful of the weekly meeting of the League's central branch at London's Devereaux pub, where "beer would flow, songs would ring out and political debate would go on till the latest hour. It was all so fulfilling; it was all so ultimately empty."[14]

Another common view is that Distributism simply proved to be wrong in both its analysis and its prescription. One writer notes that while Belloc and Chesterton saw freedom as a function of owning the means of production, "modern workers think of it as a function of consumption"; they are less interested in where goods and services come from "and more interested in how to protect their ability to purchase them.[15] According to biographer Robert Speaight, Belloc's prophecies of a "Servile State" failed to understand how the state itself, rather than some capitalist oligarchy, "would become the more or less benevolent slave-owner," while the rich would in fact be "progressively impoverished by successive governments."[16] W. H. Auden underscores "the basic contradiction" in the Distributism advanced by Roman Catholics such as Belloc and Chesterton: it could only be achieved in a crowded, industrial nation such as Britain if the population was first reduced through strenuous birth control, which the Chesterbelloc fiercely opposed.[17]

Most analysts also stress how "the Belloc tail wagged the Chesterton dog," with the former leading the latter "into wasting his genius in the deserts of politics and the arid soil of Distributism."[18] Indeed, in 1923 Chesterton did write to Belloc that "you were the founder and father of this mission; we [others] were the converts but you were the missionary."[19] In his able biography of Belloc, John P. McCarthy concurs that Chesterton "was very greatly indebted to Belloc in the formation of his opinions" and "should be regarded more as the articulate disciple in these matters."[20] Christopher Hollis adds that whenever Chesterton addressed Distributism, "he spoke only as an obedient disciple, repeating what Belloc told him to repeat."[21] According to Coren, though, Chesterton's death in 1936 "signified the end of the [Distributist] philosophy, if that is what it was," adding: "The only important debate is concerned with how much the League and the magazine distracted [Chesterton] from the more important vocation of his books, and serious articles."[22]

This chapter takes issue with all of the above assertions and conclusions. To begin with, Distributism actually displayed impressive levels of clarity, coherence, and detail. In terms of specific policies, Chesterton, Belloc, and their allies ran rings around the orthodox economists and the standard party platforms of the 1920s and 1930s, not to mention those of the early twenty-first century. Second, despite his polite deference to Belloc, Chesterton was at least as responsible as his elder for developing Distributism as a compelling Third Way model and for providing concrete policy ideas. Third, rather than wasting his talents in this arena, Chesterton produced some of his most important and enduring work under the Distributist banner. Fourth, Distributism did not die in 1936. Rather, it inspired—directly and indirectly—key aspects of the post–World War II reconstruction of Britain, the United States, Canada, and Australia. Fifth, Belloc's analysis of the "Servile State" was not only correct in his time; it also provides the surest path to understanding the peculiar and dominant "state capitalism" of the early twenty-first century. Finally, even the chaotic debates and beer-driven camaraderie of the old Distributist League continue to inspire new generations of young adults as a model of political and intellectual engagement.

The Catholic Imperative

The origin of Distributism lies in the papal encyclical *Rerum Novarum*, issued by Leo XIII in 1891. As a 1931 editorial in *G. K.'s Weekly* summarized:

> This encyclical, in its few but brilliant pages of wisdom and exhortation, presents so clear an outline of that so-cial philosophy we call Distributism . . . that no excuse is necessary to Distributists of any creed for reminding them of a book so bound up with their aims and so characterized by humanity and vision.[23]

Acknowledging this debt to *Rerum Novarum*, the English priest Vincent McNabb declared: "For us Catholics, the Distributist State is not something we discuss, but something we *have to* propagate and institute."[24] As Coren explains, "Distributism was in [Chesterton's] eyes a *natural* and *inevitable* extension of his own religion."[25]

Rerum Novarum was the first of the great Catholic social en-cyclicals, usually remembered for its attention to the plight of industrial workers, its rejection of both unbridled capitalism and socialism, and its readiness to engage the modern age with a positive program of reform. However, it can also be read as a manifesto for the restoration of property and an agrarian return to the land.

Early in the document, Leo XIII explains that it is reason which distinguishes human creatures from the brutes, and "which renders a human being human." It is because of this endowment that man alone has a right "to possess things not merely for temporary and momentary use, as other living things do, but to have and to hold them in stable and permanent possession." The pope notes that the careful study of "the laws of nature" affirms this "foundation of the division of property [among men], and the practice of all ages has consecrated the principle of private ownership, as being pre-eminently in conformity with human nature."[26]

Moreover, this fundamental right to property holds a special relation to the land. As Leo writes: "the earth, even though apportioned among private owners, ceases not thereby to minister to the needs of all, in as much as there is not one who does not sustain life from what the land produces." This agrarian theory of value means that those who do not own the soil still contribute their labor; hence, "all *human subsistence* is derived either from labor on *one's own land*, or from some toil, some calling, which is paid for either in *the produce of the land itself*, or in that which is exchanged *for what the land brings forth*." This foundation of the true human economy on agriculture also explains Leo's embrace of the "labor property" theorem favored by agrarians: namely, that land should belong to those who physically work it. As he writes:

> Now, when man thus turns the activity of his mind and the strength of his body toward procuring the fruits of nature, by such act he makes his own that portion of nature's field which he cultivates—that portion on which he leaves, as it were, the impress of his personality; and it cannot but be *just that he should possess that portion as his very own*, and have a right to hold it *without any one being justified in violating that right*.[27]

Leo's clarion call for small-scale, peasant agriculture implicitly declared over 80 percent of Europe's land—circa 1891—to be held *unjustly* by absentee landlords; in England, the figure was over 90 percent. In effect, *Rerum Novarum* stands as a call for peaceful agrarian revolution.

The pope also grounds the right to own property in the family, the God-ordained cell of society. He underscores that no human action or law can "abolish the natural and original right of marriage, nor in any way limit the chief and principle purpose of marriage ordained by God's authority from the beginning: 'Increase and multiply.'" Using language that Chesterton would later adopt, Leo continues: "Hence we have the family, the 'society' of a man's house—a society very small, one must admit, but none the less a true society, and one older than any State." From this, the natural family gains duties and rights "peculiar to itself" and "quite independent of the State." Indeed, the "right to property," already shown to belong "naturally" to the individual, must also belong "to a man in his capacity of head of a family." This right becomes "all the stronger in proportion as the human person receives a wider extension in the family group." The Pope emphasizes that the "most sacred law of nature [is] that a father should provide food and all necessaries for those whom he has begotten." It is also "natural" that he want those children who "carry on . . . his personality" to be provisioned against want and misery. Leo concludes: "in no other way can a father effect this except by the ownership of productive property."[28]

And so, the pope declares the first duty of the state to be the safeguarding of justly held private property. The "great labor question" facing the modern era could not be solved except by acknowledging "that private ownership must be held sacred and inviolable." Most observers see this statement as a rejection of socialism. It is surely that, but it is also much more. For *Rerum Novarum* urges that the law "*should favor ownership, and its policy should be to induce as many as possible of the people to become owners.*" By ownership, moreover, Leo means above all the possession of land. As he writes: "If working people can be encouraged to look forward to obtaining *a share in the land*, the consequence will be that the gulf between vast wealth and sheer poverty will be bridged over, and the respective classes will be brought nearer to one another."[29] In short, the crafting of a society based on small property, particularly in land, becomes the Catholic solution to the modern industrial crisis.

Chesterton, the Missionary

While Belloc was clearly struggling with questions of liberty and property during the inaugural decade of the twentieth century, the first book-length treatment of Distributist themes actually came from Chesterton in 1910: *What's Wrong with the World*. Since 1901, Chesterton had been wrestling with the implications of *Rerum Novarum*, both in his columns for the liberal *Daily News* and in articles for the eclectic journal *New Age*, edited by the "guild socialist" A. R. Orage.[30]

With Belloc, Chesterton shaped his ideas in partial reaction to the dominant "progressive" ideologists of his day: H. G. Wells, George Bernard Shaw, and Sidney and Beatrice Webb. Wells thought the common man to be fairly hopeless. To rescue the young from incompetent parents, he believed that "the community as a whole" should take charge of their upbringing, with the parents consigned to "celibate labor establishments." Instead of private property acting to promote social hygiene, Wells thought an active eugenics policy would lead to "the development of a healthy, intelligent, and adaptable race." Shaw agreed. The Webbs, meanwhile, wanted to use public welfare policy to "shape up" the poor, through everything from public regulation of wages, hours, and working conditions to the founding of Reformatory Detention Colonies, where the poor could serve society with efficiency. As Belloc quipped, "'Running' the poor is [the Webbs'] hobby, and the occupation of the ample leisure which their own position as capitalists affords them."[31]

Where Wells and Shaw would improve the masses through eugenic breeding and the Webbs through state controls, Chesterton proposed a different model. As Margaret Canovan explains, he

> built upon a sympathy with the deeply-rooted emo-
> tions that cluster around the home and the homeland:
> the love of the ordinary man not only for his family,
> but for his home; the longing for a little domain of
> one's own, whether it be a peasant's land, or a suburban
> clerk's garden, or even a slum dweller's back yard.[32]

Applying *Rerum Novarum* to English politics brought Chesterton into conflict with his coreligionists. The more conservative Catholics had taken the encyclical as "a general confirmation of the established order." They emphasized the document's condemnation of socialism and ignored its critical dissection of capitalism as well as its agrarian claims.[33] In response, Chesterton would emphasize the "exceedingly radical" implications of arguing that men and women are wonderfully different, that public life exists to defend private life, that property secures liberty, and that "all political and social efforts must be devoted to securing the good of the family": the basic lessons of *Rerum Novarum*.[34]

An unsigned review of *What's Wrong with The World* appeared in the July 30, 1910, issue of the *Saturday Review*. Despite a slightly cynical tone, it ably captures the thesis of the book:

> Plainly stated, the whole wrong is that Jones has not
> all that he should have. Jones, being the normal man,
> wants a home, a wife, some children, and a bit of prop-
> erty. At present, he may have none of these things. His
> home is often a flat or a tenement; his wife is often a
> wage-earner, his children are not his own, for the State
> can have their hair cut because his wife is not permit-

ted to keep them clean; and as for property—England is a "feudal" country, so that a poor man's back garden belongs to somebody else. What is wrong with this world is precisely this—that modern politics, economics and ethics all conspire to keep Jones from having what he ought to have.[35]

Echoing Leo XIII, Chesterton opens his defense of property by appealing to "the principle of domesticity: the ideal house, the happy family, the holy family of history." With irony, he notes that "the cultured class," the progressive intelligentsia, "is shrieking to be let out of the decent home" in favor of a sensual, postfamilial order. Meanwhile, "the working class is shouting to be let into it." In a powerful passage directly inspired by *Rerum Novarum*, Chesterton celebrates "the free family," declaring: "It may be said that this institution of the home is the one anarchist institution. That is to say, it is older than law and stands outside the state. By its nature it is refreshed or corrupted by indefinable forces of custom or kinship."[36]

In the early twentieth century, new distempers threatened the free family, including the advocacy of easy divorce. Chesterton tackles this head on, asserting that "the success of the marriage comes after the failure of the honeymoon." Underscoring the real nature of marriage, Chesterton adds that "[a]ll human vows, laws, and contracts are so many ways of surviving with success this breaking point, this instant of potential surrender." He asserts that the man and the woman in a marriage are "one flesh," even if not "one spirit": "Man is a quadraped."[37]

The same "upper class philosophies" of Wells, Shaw, and the Webbs threatened the physical home, as well. Under their sway, wrote Chesterton, "the average man has really become bewildered about the goal of his efforts, and his efforts, therefore, grow feebler and feebler. His simple notion of having a home of his own is derided as bourgeois, as sentimental, or as despicably

Christian." Feminists, meanwhile, condemned the mother in the home as a dependent ornament who yearned to be free.[38]

Chesterton responds with the truth "that to the moderately poor the home is the only place of liberty. Nay, it is the only place of anarchy." Coining a wonderful phrase, he labels the family home a "chamber of liberty." Chesterton notes that the average worker does not want a semi-attached house nor a flat in a high-rise building. "He wants . . . a separate house," because the "idea of *earthly contact* and foundation, as well as an idea of separation and independence, is a part of this instructive human picture." In this private home tied to the soil, human life finds fulfillment:

> As every normal man desires a woman, and children born of a woman, every normal man desires a house of his own to put them into. . . . [H]e wants an objective and visible kingdom, a fire at which he can cook what food he likes, a door he can open to what friends he chooses.

Chesterton concludes that to "give nearly everybody ordinary houses would please nearly everybody; that is what I assert without apology."[39]

More broadly, he notes that for most persons "the idea of artistic creation can only be expressed by an idea unpopular in present discussions—the idea of property." The average man or woman cannot produce a great painting or a memorable sculpture. Together, however, they can imprint their personalities on the earth, on their homes, and on their small workshops. "Property is merely the art of the democracy," Chesterton richly intones. "It means that every man should have something that he can shape in his own image, as he is shaped in the image of heaven."[40]

Belloc, the Prophet

In his inaugural book-length treatment of Distributist themes, Belloc explores in depth the reasons for the disappearance of England's "chambers of liberty" and other forms of private property. Appearing in 1912, *The Servile State* offers an unexpected and fairly complicated argument. Belloc asserts

> [t]hat our free modern society in which the means of production are owned by a few being necessarily in unstable equilibrium, it is tending to reach a condition of stable equilibrium by the establishment of compulsory labor legally enforceable upon those who do not own the means of production for the advantage of those who do.[41]

Belloc rephrases his thesis for the second edition of the book, stating that "the effect of socialist doctrine upon capitalist society is to produce a third thing different from either of its two begetters—to wit, the Servile State." By servile, he means precisely slavery, where "an unfree majority of non-owners" work for the gain of "a free minority of owners." Where capitalism has held sway, this "reestablishment of slavery" is "a necessary development," and nowhere more so than in England.[42]

Behind these startling assertions lie key definitions. By capitalism, Belloc means a system of oligarchic monopoly, where ownership of land and capital is confined to a minority of free citizens, while the property-less majority form a proletariat dependent solely on wages. By "Servile State," he means political, economic, and social arrangements under which a majority of families and individuals "are constrained by positive law to labor for the advantage of other families and individuals." In this circumstance, wages are supplemented by state regulations and benefits insuring minimal "sufficiency and security." All the same, it involves "reestablishing the slave."[43]

Belloc provides a lengthy historical narrative on how modern England fell into the new slavery. Here he borrows arguments from R. H. Tawney's *The Agrarian Problem in the Sixteenth Century,* which chronicled the opening blows against England's free yeomanry.[44] Slavery, Belloc notes, has been commonplace in human history; liberty, the exception. Certainly, between 500 and 1000 A.D. the European peoples took slavery for granted. Poverty "made the slave," as indigent men sold themselves into slavery as an alternative to starvation. Slaves and masters alike accepted the system as a given.

However, in the bosom of the Western Christian church, freedom slowly spread. By 900 A.D. or so, the sale of men had come to an end. A century later, slaves on country villas became serfs, with compulsory labor replaced by a fixed payment of produce and with the peasants gaining customary rights to the use of land. "Then, as now," Belloc the agrarian relates, "the soil and its fixtures were the basis of all wealth," and this wealth was once again effectively in the control of those who worked the soil. In the towns, meanwhile, self-governing guilds emerged to control the production, quality, and pricing of goods and services. This "distributive system" of cooperative bodies worked to prevent emergence of an economic oligarchy. As Belloc explains, such "restraints upon liberty were restraints designed for the preservation of [a broader] liberty."[45]

Alas, Belloc argues, this medieval Distributist order was replaced by "the dreadful moral anarchy . . . which goes by the name of capitalism." England, once a land of owners, became by 1912 a land of property-less proletarians, with one-third of the people indigent and nineteen of every twenty dispossessed of land and capital. The cause of this change, Belloc stresses, was not the invention of new machines and the rise of industry. Rather, monopoly capitalism derived from "the deliberate action of men, evil will in a few and apathy of will among the many." And it began in the sixteenth, not the eighteenth century.

The key act, in Belloc's view, was the seizure of monastic lands by the English crown in the 1530s and 1540s. These properties, about 30 percent of England's arable land, quickly fell into the hands of the rural squires, who already held another 30 percent. Using legal devices such as the statute of frauds and enclosures, this landed oligarchy further suppressed and destroyed the English yeomanry over the next two centuries. By 1700, England was a land of plutocrats and protetarians. When the great mechanical inventions arrived, the rural oligarchy won control of industry and its wealth as well. Discoveries that "would have blest and enriched mankind" instead reinforced the sharp division between owners and proles.[46]

Belloc stresses, however, that "the Capitalist state is unstable" and therefore best seen as "a transitory phase" between two stable forms of society. The strains in capitalist society come partly from the conflict between the moral theories of liberty on which the state reposes and the reality of class division and exploitation. They also come from the insecurity to which capitalism condemns the mass of people. As Belloc writes, "[i]f you left men completely free under a capitalist system, there would be so heavy a mortality from starvation as would dry up the sources of labor." Indeed, "the system would break down from the death of children and out-o-works and of women." From the Elizabethan poor laws through the work houses and the Speenhamland system of child allowances to the Poor Law of 1834, capitalism used "non-capitalist methods" to keep alive the protelariat.[47]

Socialists propose a collectivist solution to this instability. They would make the state the owner of all productive capital. However, Belloc emphasizes the difficulties of collectivization, including the impossibility of real confiscation and the failed economies consequent to state control over industry. Instead, Belloc believes that the capitalist owners and the state were cutting a different deal, one creating the Servile State: "Subject the proletarian, as a proletarian, and because he is a proletarian, to special laws. Clothe me, the capitalist, as a capitalist, and because I am a capitalist, with special converse duties under those laws." Out of this resurrection of status, the capitalists would gain a sure hold on their property and wealth. Although moving "from free proletarianism to servitude," the workers would settle for "security and sufficiency."[48]

Some have interpreted Belloc's Servile State as meaning simply the welfare state, with its cradle-to-grave benefits such as health care and food stamps.[49] This is surely part of what Belloc meant. But he also implies something more, a merger of government and monopoly capital into a "corporate state" or "state capitalism." Under this system, private capitalists would be better protected from disorder and dissent than when they were dependent on voluntary efforts, while workers would be confirmed in their completely servile status.[50]

Belloc identifies the signs of the Servile State's emergence in the early twentieth century. He sees students in the modern state schools "brought up . . . definitely and hopelessly proletarian"; they are trained to see property as unattainable for their ilk and to "think of themselves as wage earners" alone. Belloc also sees a common thread to new laws and policies involving employers' liability (for employee accidents), workman's compensation, unemployment and sickness insurance, and the fixing of a minimum wage. In place of independent bargaining between two free men, these are fixed arrangements between owners and nonowners, measures that lock the latter into wage-earning servility. The author states that such legislation "would not exist in a society where property was well divided." Instead, signs of incipient slavery grow, for the converse of a minimum wage is compulsory labor, and Belloc predicts the forming of labor colonies for the recalcitrant.[51] Still, as the new order sets in, the internal strains of the capitalist era are relaxed, "and the community will settle down upon the servile basis which was its foundation before the advent of the Christian faith, from which that faith slowly weaned it, and to which in the decay of that faith it naturally returns."[52]

The only other option, Belloc states, is the re-creation of the property state. This entails actions that would redistribute ownership from the few to the many—that is, a deliberate restoration of the Distributist order as found in late-medieval Europe. In this book, though, Belloc provides little guidance on how to pursue this end. Rather, he worries that the instincts necessary for the survival of private property are already too far gone: "Will men want to own? Will officials, administrators, and lawmakers be able to shake off the power which under capitalism seems normal to the rich? . . . Can I discover any relics of the cooperative instinct among such men?"[53] He offers little hope for the England of his day.

However, in a parallel set of essays also published in 1912 and appearing in the *Oxford and Cambridge Review*, Belloc lays out concrete reforms that could restore property to families. He calls on the state to act "continually as the protector and nourisher of the small man" through measures such as differentiated corporate taxes that favor new and small companies and the state subsidization of bonds purchased by low-income households.[54] He would return to and expand on these ideas in his 1936 essay *The Restoration of Property*.

One compelling idea, though, appears only in the 1912 version of the essay. Here, Belloc answers the critics of Distributism who mock talk of re-creating a peasantry. Belloc replies that he did not expect the first experiments in restoring ownership to occur among agricultural holders. Rather,

> the great field . . . for experiments of this kind, paradoxical as it may sound, is *the suburban field*. . . . [T]here is a universal tendency making for private ownership of houses and small plots just outside our great urban cen-

> ters, and here *a revolution upon a great scale could be effected*
> if the credit of the community were called into play.[55]

This was a prophecy that would be fulfilled, albeit in unexpected places.

The Kingdom of the Home

By the mid-1920s Distributism drew mounting attention, a consequence in part of the crisis afflicting international capitalism. Hyperinflation, rising trade barriers, agricultural depression, unemployment: all pointed to the failure of the pre-1914 liberal order to recover after the Great War. All the same, Chesterton faced scathing criticism for his fanciful theories and their lack of specifics. As Maisie Ward remarks, "With bland disregard of the breakdown of their own system, the orthodox economists were challenging him to establish the flawlessness of his."[56]

One result was *The Outline of Sanity* (1926), Chesterton's most complete Distributist treatise. Like Belloc, he offers careful distinctions. "If capitalism means private property, I am capitalist," he reports. "If capitalism means capital, everyone is capitalist." However, Chesterton argues that the label now held a narrower meaning. A "relatively small" class of capitalists possess "so much of the capital" that "a very large majority" of the citizens must serve these capitalists for a wage. Such an exercise of monopoly "is neither private nor enterprising," he adds. Indeed, it "exists to prevent private enterprise." Meanwhile, socialism would make "the corporate unity of society" responsible for all economic processes, representing "an extreme enthusiasm for authority." Distributism, in contrast, is premised on the family, the kingdom of the home. Because capitalists and socialists "dislike the independence of the kingdom, they are against property. Because they dislike the loyalty of that kingdom, they are against marriage." Distributists alone "insist in the full sense that the average respectable citizen ought to have something to rule." Again alone, and because of this respect for property, Distributists have the unique right to be called democratic.[57]

Chesterton notes that his critics have called a policy of small distributed property "impossible," a fantasy, due to the "Law of Rent" and other devices that make concentration inevitable. "It is true that I believe in fairy tales," he retorts, "in the sense that I marvel so much at what does exist that I am the readier to admit what might." More directly, he asserts that "the monopolist momentum is not irresistible," adding: "It may be very difficult for modern people to imagine a world in which men are not generally admired for covetousness and crushing their neighbours; but I assure them that such strange patches of an earthly paradise do really remain on earth."[58]

All the same, Chesterton acknowledges the difficulty of the situation. He accepts the historical account laid out in more detail by Belloc, concluding that "England became a capitalist country because it had long been an oligarchic country." In recent decades, the "passion for incessant and ruthless buying and selling goes along with the extreme inequality of men too rich or too poor." After passing a certain point, "the broken fragments of property" prove to be "easily devoured." In terms of regimentation and centralization, "capitalism has done all that socialism threatened to do." Under prevailing trends, "[t]here is nothing in front but a flat wilderness of standardization either by Bolshevism or Big Business."[59]

Indeed, by the mid-1920s, owners of the great businesses in England had themselves abandoned liberal economics. Instead of believing that if men were left to bargain individually the public would automatically benefit, they now pleaded with workers not to strike "in the interests of the public." Chesterton quips: "the only original case for capitalism collapses entirely, if we have to ask either party to go on for the good of the public." Instead, "ordinary conservatives are falling back" on Communist arguments "without knowing it." Add in the near-disappearance of English agriculture, and it was clear that English leaders for almost a century had committed their nation to "new and enormous experiments," including, in Chesterton's words:

- "to make their own nation an eternal debtor to a few rich men";
- "to driving food out of their own country in the hope of buying it back again from the ends of the earth";
- "to losing every type of moderate prosperity . . . till there was no independence without luxury and no labour without ugliness";

And all of this "hanging on a thread of alien trade which [grows] thinner and thinner."[60]

Great trusts, or monopoly combines, had also been allowed to form. For a long time, capitalist apologists denied that such trusts could arise within a free market. By the 1920s, Chesterton reports, "[t]hey talk as if the Trusts had always been a part of the British Constitution, not to mention the Solar System." Yet such adamancy reveals weakness. It is dangerous, he says, to suppose "the capitalist conquest more complete than it is."[61]

In place of these perilous and failing experiments, Chesterton calls for the restoration of property to the masses. Following *Rerum Novarum*, he grounds hope for renewal in families: "As each . . . family finds again the real experience of private property, it will become a centre of influence, a mission," and a movement. Furthermore, as in *Rerum Novarum*, this mission would necessarily involve the creation of a free peasantry, a form of "moderate equality," a "peasant state" natural to humanity. Chesterton summons "the whole of the household religion, or what remains of it, to offer resistance to the destructive discipline of [monopoly] industrial capitalism." He counsels, "do anything, however small, that will prevent the completion of the work of capitalist combinations." Save one small farm; shop at one small store. "For it is the essence of [capitalism's] enormous and unnatural effort that a small failure is as big as a big failure."[62]

More broadly, Chesterton offers a practical and detailed action agenda. It may be outlined as follows:

• To support the small retailer and the little shop, boycott the large department stores. This should be as easy as boycotting "shops selling instruments of torture or poisons for private use in the home."

• To break up monopoly corporations, support the gradual extension of profit sharing or the steady transfer of ownership to worker guilds. "[A]ny reversal of the rush to concentrate property will be an improvement on the present state of things."

• To redistribute land and other properties, tax contracts "so as to discourage the sale of small property to big proprietors and encourage the break up of big property among small proprietors." A model would be Ireland's Wyndham Act of 1903, which successfully transferred farms from absentee landlords to peasants.

• To divide property fairly within families, destroy primogeniture or inheritance preferences for the first-born son.

• To defend the poor against the great, provide the former free legal services.

• To protect certain experiments in small property, provide subsidies and employ tariffs, "even local tariffs."

• To break up the trusts, mobilize prosecutors to enforce laws banning "cornering," "dumping," and loan-sharking. Put scheming capitalists in jail, for "private property ought to be protected against public crime."

• To encourage agriculture, take schools which have been teaching "town things to country people who did not want to learn them" and instead teach "country things to town people who do want to learn them."

• To preserve residual healthy sentiments, end urban renewal plans (such as the infamous "Limehouse project")[63] that destroy the jealously held fences, chicken coops, and small gardens of city dwellers and move them into sterile high-rise apartments. "We should seize on these [recalcitrant] slum-dwellers as if they were infant prodigies. . . . We should see in them the seed and living principle of a real spontaneous revival of the countryside."

• To make peace with the machines, family ownership is to be preferred, followed by cooperative control, or—if necessary—ownership by equal shares. In order to "create the experience of small property," Chesterton happily accepts "any help that science and machinery can give in creating small property."

• To decentralize industry, cheapen electricity and expand access grids, "which might lead to many little workshops."

• To decentralize transportation, discourage the railroads and favor the automobile. In praising the Ford Model T, Chesterton marvels that "nobody seems to notice how this popularization of motoring . . . really is a complete contradiction to the fatalistic talk about inevitable combination and concentration." In fact, after the tyranny of the railroads, "the free and solitary traveler is returning before our very eyes . . . having recovered to some extent the freedom of the King's highway in the manner of Merry England."

• To empty the cities, favor the suburbs. "[I]f possessing a Ford car means rejoicing in a field of corn or clover, in a fresh landscape and a free atmosphere, it may be the beginning of many things. . . . It may be, for instance, . . . the beginning of the cottage."[64]

The alternative to such an agenda, Chesterton warns, is the final merger of socialism and capitalism: "believing only in combination, they will themselves combine." In place of Belloc's language about the Servile State, Chesterton more usefully describes "the new sort of Business Government," an emerging unity of "collectivist" and "ordinary commercial" orders. Already, "[p]rivate things are . . . public in the worst sense of the word; that is, they are personal and dehumanized. Public things are already private in the worst sense of that word; that is, they are mysterious and secretive and largely corrupt." As capitalism and socialism consummate their merger, this "new sort of Business Government will combine everything that is bad in all the plans for a better world. . . . There will be nothing but a loathsome thing called Social Service."[65]

A Reactionary Revolution

Belloc's *The Restoration of Property* appeared a decade after Chesterton's tome. While fully compatible with the latter's direction and theme, Belloc approaches the task of explaining Distributism in a different way. Where Chesterton exuded a relative optimism, Belloc is pessimistic: "The evil has gone so far that . . . the creation of new and effective immediate machinery is impossible." At best, "it is not quite impossible to start the beginnings of a change."[66]

Joseph Pearce labels the result "essentially libertarian."[67] This is correct in its estimation of Belloc's love of true liberty, but misleading given his resort to massive state intervention. John P. McCarthy sees in Belloc's scheme "a people's capitalism."[68] This is true, if capitalism means property, but it is also misleading given the historical and linguistic context. Belloc himself calls his project "a reactionary revolution," one mounted against "Capitalism, and its product, Communism." The immediate task was "forwarding the spirit of that reaction in a society which has almost forgotten what property and its concomitant freedom means."[69]

Following both Leo XIII and Chesterton, Belloc opens with an appeal to the household as the foundation of liberty. "The family is ideally free," he writes, "when it fully controls all the means necessary for the production of such wealth as it should consume for normal living." While this ideal freedom would necessarily be tempered by a natural specialization in trades and reasonable state regulation, the family "retains its freedom, so long as the social structure, made up of families similarly free, exercises its effect through customs and laws consonant to its spirit." Such households enjoy "widely distributed property." This is the Distributist state.[70]

However, "widespread property has been lost" in England, with society falling "into the diseased condition known as 'Industrial Capitalism.'" The resulting "insecurity and insufficiency" now led either toward communism or—more likely—the Servile State. In the latter, the "masses are kept alive, they are taught by a subsidy in childhood, treated by a subsidy in illness, and maintained by a subsidy in old age, widowhood, and incapacity from accident."

The only other option was to restore economic freedom; to do so, paradoxically, the powers of the state must be summoned. Belloc reasons that since capitalism evoked "all the powers of the state" to create servile conditions, "we must [now] avail ourselves of the same methods." Restoring property requires "a deliberate reversal of economic tendencies," for market processes left unchecked lead to monopoly control of the means of production. Hence, "[w]ell-divided property will not spring up of itself in a Capitalist society. It must be artificially fostered."[71]

Belloc offers seven reasons why monopoly capitalism wins out over well-distributed property in the middle and long runs:

1. *Overhead.* "The larger unit is in proportion less expensive than the smaller in management, rent, [and] upkeep."

2. *Information.* The larger unit is better able to purchase "machinery . . . and information." It also dominates advertising, "one of the worst plagues of English modern life."

3. *Credit.* The larger unit can borrow more easily than the smaller one. It can better bargain for special interest rates, and is more likely to see the bank throwing "good money after bad."

4. *Dumping.* "The larger institution can undersell the smaller one at a loss, until the smaller one is imperiled or killed."

5. *Capital.* "[Y]ou cannot tempt small capital to make the beginnings of serious accumulation at the rates which are sufficient for large capital."

6. *Corruption.* "Plutocracy once established will corrupt the legislature so that laws will be made in its favor."

7. *Justice.* "The cost of recovering a small debt is out of all proportion to the cost of recovering a large one."[72]

In response, Belloc summons the state to counter these inevitable tendencies with positive action. He seeks to restore the small cultivator, wholesaler, shopkeeper, and artisan. He wants to divide large properties into smaller units. And he desires to confirm such division by defensive institutions. His specific policy proposals include:

• To restore the small shop, use differential taxation against chain stores (no more than a dozen shops) and department stores (he specifically cites Harrods) and also employ licensing to limit the number of products that each shop can sell;

• To decentralize distribution, apply a turnover tax to large wholesalers, with the money raised put into a "Guild Credit Union" to finance new small suppliers;

• To restore craftsmen, subsidize "the small artisan at the expense of Big Business." In addition, bring back the trade guilds, "chartered and established by positive law."

• To break up large industrial combines, change the legal rules that favor consolidation. Where existing laws encourage centralized steam and water power, electrical power offers a decentralized alternative: "A differential tax on power used would effect this." Where amalgamation is not the result of technology, "[w]e must penalize amalgamation and support division of units" through differential taxation. If shares are to be divided, "we should aim at creating the largest possible number of shareholders" and prevent the accumulation of large blocks of stock, again through differential taxation. The proceeds of this tax would subsidize "purchase by the smaller holders."

• To guarantee popular corporate governance, a supermajority of stockholders would be needed for key decisions, so that a "small proportion of individual shareholders" could block a policy change. Moreover, no corporation or affiliation of companies could buy shares in another company.

• To encourage agrarian resettlement, "agricultural land shall be treated differently from urban land." There must be "a radical difference in the burdens imposed upon the land occupied, as land (according to our view) should be occupied, by a human family living thereon, and land occupied by others from whom the owners draw tribute."

• To encourage subsistence agriculture, where each family largely lives off its own produce, the "peasantry must be privileged as against the diseased society around it." This new peasantry "must begin as a social luxury" and "like all luxuries, be extravagantly paid for." This means that the burdens of taxation and borrowing laid upon the peasantry must be light . . . or nonexistent. It must be easy for the small holder to buy land from the rich, and difficult to sell the other way.

• To encourage urban home ownership, "there ought to be a simple rule: every lease should automatically contain the power of purchase by installment."[73]

• To encourage easy credit, the state should create and subsidize "chartered cooperative banks" or credit unions under local control.

Belloc's almost promiscuous use of "differential" and progressive taxation to achieve his goals may well frighten the modern libertarian. However, the details of his plan are interesting. "High taxation is incompatible with the general institution of property," he remarks. Truly high progressive rates of taxation are possible only in "a society like our own in which small property has decayed." Put another way, "high taxation destroys the Middle Class. It dries up the stream by which a middle class is brought into existence and maintained. It breeds plutocracy." As he notes, the high taxes of his era were due entirely to the waging of war "financed by bank credit" and to "the increase of State Socialism [the welfare state] for the purpose of guaranteeing capitalism against a revolt of a proletariat." Meanwhile, Belloc's transitional scheme for moving from monopoly capitalism to Distributism would use outrageously high tax rates (as an "outrageous" example, he cites 25 percent—actually a modest figure by twenty-first century standards!) only for a time. Once widely distributed property was the rule in society and *the need for a welfare state had been eliminated*, he calculates that the state could survive on a "flax tax" of just *2 percent!*[74]

Roll together the policy ideas of both Chesterton and Belloc, and one has a remarkably complete and integrated political program. It could be labelled unrealistic, but complaints over its incoherence or lack of specificity simply hold no water.

Moreover, during the early 1920s, Chesterton and Belloc entered real political battles. For example, they fought "furiously" in the "London Omnibus War," favoring the small, private bus companies that challenged the monopoly held by Lord Ashfield's London General Omnibus Transportation Company.[75] After Chesterton founded G. K.'s Weekly in 1925 to promote Distributist thinking, the little journal poured out an impressive series of commentaries applying Distributist principles to concrete issues. In an editorial on "Hitler as Distributist," the Weekly examined new German policies favoring births and stay-at-home mothers. Was the family truly valued by the Nazis? No, "the purpose is not to create a primary political unit; the purpose is to create the birth-rate," to manufacture human fodder for war.[76] Concerning structural unemployment, the magazine proposed an ingenious scheme to turn unemployment insurance benefits into a stipend that would settle affected families on twenty-five acres and provide them livestock, seed, and fifteen months of salary, so getting them started as property-holders.[77] Turning to "The Drink Problem," G. K.'s Weekly proposed reforms "so that the supply [of alcoholic beverages] may be as good, cheap, and wholesome as possible." Specifics included a "demand" that all state restrictions on the manufacture, sale, and consumption of alcohol imposed since 1914 be scrapped; that the government issue many more licenses for "publick houses"; and that taxes on liquor, wine, and beer be slashed.[78]

Legend or Libation?

Speaking of beer, the Distributists' reputation for excessive consumption also needs clarification. That meetings of the Distributist League were occasions for spirited debates on issues both practical and "deeply theoretical" (e.g., "Should we abolish the machines?"), for camaraderie, and for "the drinking of a good deal of beer" seems clear. Despite being a cofounder of the League, though, Belloc rarely attended these events and kept his distance from the Leaguers. He particularly disliked the beer-swilling legend. Slated to discuss "monopoly" at Essex Hall, he heard the chairman of the event announce that "Mr. Belloc will speak about beer, about which he knows a good deal." He rose and, addressing the reporters present, snarled: "Let me warn you gentlemen, that if any of your masters prints any vulgar sneer about me and beer, they will live to rue it."[79]

Chesterton, however, obviously favored the convivial atmosphere of the Distributist League, which he served as president. During these "Devereux Nights . . . politics and economics were put aside in favour of song and good fellowship." Chesterton particularly relished the League's Annual General Meeting, when provincial delegates joined London members for a business session followed by a grand dinner at Carr's Restaurant in Aldwych. As Brocard Sewell recalled, "[a]fter the meal, and the customary toasts and speeches, the evening would be rounded off with song. Chesterton joined in all the choruses, and thoroughly enjoyed the whole affair." The songs were mostly originals written by the Distributists themselves, such as "King Solomon's Wives":

> King Solomon had ten thousand wives
> In his house of cedar wood.
> There was Sheba's queen, and Helen of Troy,
> And Little Red Riding Hood.

But whether their skins were white as milk,

Or black as a chimney-sweep,

There were no flies on the shy gazelles

King Solomon used to keep.

Yo ho! Yo ho! Yo ho!

Then send the drink around.

And here's to every fancy lass

In London to be found!

Such details help explain why few women attended Distributist events. All the same, "they were gatherings of friends," [80] and they exerted a powerful hold on later, sympathetic imaginations.

What Legacy?

If drinking songs were all that Distributism left behind, then the conventional wisdom about the movement's frivolity would be sound. In truth, Distributism has had real, even profound effects on a number of nations, and it stands to this day as a powerful tool of analysis and a compelling program of reform.

In Great Britain as early as 1916, Prime Minister David Lloyd George adopted Chestertonian language to promise soldiers in the trenches "three acres and a cow" after the war. While he failed to deliver, supporting only a few chicken farms, Britain's Conservative Party adopted Distributist language and goals after World War II with greater effect. At the 1946 party conference, Winston Churchill rejected the establishment of a socialist state controlling the means of production. Instead, he said,

> Our Conservative aim is to build a *property-owning-democracy,* both independent and interdependent. In this I include profit-sharing schemes in suitable indus-

> tries and intimate consultation between employers and
> wage earners. In fact we seek so far as possible to make
> the status of the wage-earner that of a partner rather
> than of an irresponsible employee . . . *Our ideal is the*
> *consenting union of millions of free, independent families and*
> *homes.*[81]

In his 1955 address to the party, Anthony Eden also extolled
"what I have many times described as a property-owning-
democracy." This ownership, he said, could "be expressed in
the home, in savings or in forms of partnership in industry."
Conservatives stood "against increased ownership of power and
property by the State. We seek ever wider ownership of power
and property by the people."[82] Even in the party's manifesto of
2005, "expanding our property-owning democracy" remains a
central theme. The Conservative focus today is on the "Right
to Buy for council tenants," "plans to boost shared ownership
schemes," and giving "social housing tenants the right to own
a share of their home."[83] Such policy ideas are right out of the
Distributist playbook.

In the United States, Distributism also had a strong and lasting effect on public policy. A key intermediary was Herbert
Agar, winner of the Pulitzer Prize for his book *The People's*
Choice (1933). For six years, he held a junior editorial position
at *G. K.'s Weekly* and absorbed the Distributist ethos. Returning to America, he crafted a 1934 essay for the *American Re-*
view titled "The Task for Conservatism." Using language borrowed directly from Belloc and Chesterton, he showed how
the American founders had believed "that a wide diffusion of
property . . . made for enterprise, for family responsibility, and
. . . for institutions that fit man's nature." During the nineteenth century, however, plutocrats despoiled small-property
holders, leaving most Americans in wage-earning "servitude."
Agar concluded that a "redistribution of property" could yet

be achieved, which would form "the root of a real conservative policy for the United States." This goal would need to be "produced artificially" and protected by special legislation. The choice was clear: "Either we restore property, or we restore slavery."[84] With homegrown American Distributists such as Ralph Borsodi, he cofounded in 1937 the monthly *Free America*, which became a mouthpiece for the cause. The journal was "the meeting ground for those who are equally opposed to finance-capitalism, communism, and fascism," with "decentralization" as its "fundamental principle."[85]

Distributist ideals even shaped key New Deal initiatives. The Subsistence Homestead program—which provided a house, garden, and five acres in villages to displaced families—drew direct inspiration from Distributist activists in England and America.[86] By 1940, more than two hundred of these federal projects were underway. Of greater long-term importance were the new housing programs that also derived from Distributist ideals. The Home Owners Loan Act of 1933 introduced a novel type of long-term, low-interest loan. By 1936, over one million mortgages of this sort had been issued. The Housing Act of 1934 "revolutionized" home financing by—as Belloc had once urged—calling into play "the credit of the community" and sparking "a revolution upon a great scale" in "the suburban field." The new Federal Housing Administration (FHA) perfected the long-term amortized mortgage with a low down payment; after World War II, FHA loans—in conjunction with their Veterans Administration counterparts—seeded the suburbanization of America. Between 1945 and 1960, the number of owner-occupied homes nearly doubled, transforming America from a land of renters into a land of owners. The same years saw a marked increase in economic equality among Americans: there were fewer of the poor and the very rich and a mighty advance by the middle class. Belloc and Chesterton would have been pleased (although the latter would probably have wisely recommended the placement of more "publick houses" in the new suburban neighborhoods).

In Canada, two Distributist Catholic priests—Jimmy Tompkins and Moses Coady—launched the Antigonish movement among the Acadian French of Nova Scotia. Focusing on cooperative marketing ventures, they organized by 1939 some 342 credit unions and 162 other co-ops, involving 20,000 members. Lobstermen, fishermen, and weavers all experienced improvements in their living standards.[87] Meanwhile, in Australia, the Campion Society of Melbourne formed in 1931 to discuss the works of Chesterton and Belloc. Among other effects, the society launched the career of B. A. Santamaria as an active Distributist. First as a rural organizer for the Catholic Social Movement, then as leader of "The Movement," which successfully countered Communist influence in the labor unions, followed by his role as an inspiration for the formation of the crucial Democratic Labour Party and its "model Distributist program," and finally as founder of the Australian Family Association, Santamaria had an undeniably significant influence on Australian life.[88]

True, efforts at the restoration of peasantries mostly failed. All the same, the results noted above by themselves lift Distributism out of the "ludicrous" and "frivolous" categories. Moreover, Belloc's concept of the Servile State and Chesterton's of the Business Government bear new relevance in the early twenty-first century. For example, leading corporate consultants such as Stewart Friedman and Jeffrey Greenhaus now argue that work-family conflicts demand a state-imposed "revolution" in gender roles. Women must be pulled more completely into the corporate world, while men must be retrained to work as caregivers. Meanwhile, the state must assume "responsibility for all children, even other people's children." Such gender engineering and fresh expansion of the welfare state are "the brave new world" lying within "the workplace revolution."[89] This would surely be a Business Government at work.

Even Belloc's seemingly extreme claim that compulsory labor would soon return has now comes true, most visibly for women. The American welfare reform of 1996, for example, ended a system that had supported poor mothers staying at home with their children. The new plan ties state benefits for mothers to mandatory work at the minimum wage: a perfect definition of the Servile State. More broadly, Sweden's Treasury Minister a few years ago dismissed a proposed monthly stipend for stay-at-home parents caring for toddlers. "Mothers at home do nothing for the state," he argued. All adults must work, for only then can the state gain tax revenue to pay for welfare benefits: again, a perfect expression of the new servility. American advocates for "equal opportunity and equal access" in the workplace agree: all able adults must work, and all nonworking dependents must receive care from "society," meaning—of course—the state.[90] On this very point, Theda Skocpol declares that "it is a myth that vibrant capitalism and adequate social supports for working families cannot go hand in hand."[91]

As Chesterton warned, when monopoly capitalism and socialism consummate their merger, nothing would remain "but a loathsome thing called Social Service." This we now have. Nor would Belloc and he have been surprised when in 2001 the Communist Party of China opened its membership to capitalists. Rather than marking the advance of liberty, this would have been seen by the two Englishmen as but deepening the slavery of atomized individuals, now dependent jointly on megacorporations for a minimum wage and on the nanny state for security and care.[92]

These developments also open a new perspective on the model of the beer-swilling Distributist League. As Michael Ffinch reports, the "influence the Distributist movement had on the generation of young men who had grown up during [World War I], but had been too young to have taken part in the fighting, cannot be overestimated."[93] The camaraderie and the celebration of something fresh in the dismal worlds of politics and economics were surely part of the attraction. As the Servile State now consolidates its triumph, perhaps a new generation of young men—joined this time also by threatened young women—might find purpose again in another "gathering of friends."

2

The Wages of Kin:
Building a Secular Family-Wage Regime

Reconciling children's needs and family liberty with the distinct roles of men and women in a competitive industrial economy has bedeviled political economists and policymakers for over two hundred years. One response was the effort by labor leaders and social theorists to construct a family-wage system, which would redirect market signals and the structure of the labor force to accommodate marriage, complementary gender roles, and the presence of children in the home. Over time, this Third Way project drew heavy critical fire from liberal economists who objected to its economic inefficiencies, from Communists who denounced its interference with history, and from feminists who pointed to the systemic discrimination against women found in the family wage. All the same, it succeeded for a while in delivering prosperity, child well-being, and family autonomy.

The Family Wage, in Theory

Classical economic theory consistently stumbled over the status of the family. Writing in the late eighteenth century, Adam Smith might have adopted the laissez-faire argument that wages should be fixed where the supply of a given skill met the demand of producers for that skill, with marriage and the presence of offspring being irrelevant. Instead, Smith recognized the familial obligations of labor, declaring it "certain" that "in order to bring up a family, the labour of the husband and wife together *must*, even in the lowest species of common labour, be able to earn something more than what is precisely necessary for their own maintenance; but in what proportion . . . I shall not take upon me to determine."[1] However, in his earlier work, *The Theory of Moral Sentiments* (1759), Smith had described "parental tenderness" as innate to the human species. Such affection, he implied, would command the respect of employers, who would adjust compensation accordingly.[2]

The more somber Thomas R. Malthus indirectly assumed the existence of a family wage. In his pamphlet condemning the child allowances paid to the indigent under England's 1799 "Speenhamland Laws," he wrote: "If the poor would continue to receive the bounties of the rich, I apprehend that it would be possible to reduce the wages of labour to what was sufficient for the support of a single man." But in the absence of state intervention, he implied that wages would in practice find a family-sustaining level.[3] David Ricardo also acknowledged the need for a family wage. In seconding Malthus's call for a repeal of Speenhamland, Ricardo argued that market wages would naturally rise to a family level: "A man's wages should, and *would* in a really good system, be sufficient not only to maintain himself and family when he is in full work, but also to enable him to lay up a provision in a Savings Bank for those extraordinary calls."[4] Like Malthus, he offered no explanation for how or why "this really good system" would emerge.

Friedrich Engels and Karl Marx, in their analysis of capitalism, denied that employers had any interest in paying a family-sustaining wage. Engels emphasized that incentives under capitalistic relations actually tended to disrupt family bonds. The introduction of machines led to the dismissal of skilled male craftsmen and their replacement "by women and even by children at one third or half of the wages earned by the men. . . . It is inevitable that if a married woman works in a factory family life is . . . destroyed."[5]

In *Capital*, Marx advanced the same argument. On the one hand, he suggested the inevitability of a family wage, arguing that "the value of labour-power was determined not only by the labour-time necessary to maintain the individual adult labourer but also by that necessary to maintain his family."[6] On the other hand, he saw that the entry of women and children into the labor force and the concurrent displacement of household production, or *proletarianization*, would diffuse the compensation for work throughout the family, thereby reducing the value supplied by each member and so destroying the basis for a family wage. But Marx failed to pursue the argument further, apparently out of discomfort over where it would lead.[7]

Writing at the end of the nineteenth century, Communist theorist Karl Kautsky described what he saw as the consequences of full capitalist industrialization: "The labor of women and children affords the additional advantage that these are less capable of resistance than men, and their introduction into the ranks of workers increases tremendously the quantity of labor that is offered for sale in the market." As a result, the labor of women and children "lowers the wages of the working man," furthering the process of proletarianization.[8]

Later liberal economists quietly admitted that the market economy made no natural accommodation to family life. John

Stuart Mill noted that wages were the most miserly where wives and children labored alongside the husband/father. He argued for legal and customary restrictions on the labor of married women and children, so that a man's wages would support "himself, a wife, and a number of children adequate to keep up the population." He also urged that lower wages be paid to unmarried women: "the minimum, in their case, is the pittance absolutely requisite for the sustenance of one human being."[9] Alfred Marshall agreed that capitalism paid no attention to family relations. "Machinery has displaced many men, but not many boys," he noted, contributing to the dissolution of the family. "The wages of women are for similar reasons rising fast relative to those of men." While this was "a great gain" for women as individuals, it was also "an injury . . . as it tempts them to neglect their duty of building up a true home, and of investing their efforts in the personal capital of their children's character and abilities."[10]

Whereas Marxists and most industrialists were content, for different reasons, to let the competitive labor market follow its course, the leadership of the laboring class in Britain sought an alternative along the lines of Mill: the creation of a "living" or "family" wage. As early as 1825, an article in *Trades Newspaper* explained:

> The labouring men of this country . . . should return to the good old plan of subsisting their wives and children on the wages of their own labour and they should demand wages high enough for this purpose. . . . By doing this, the capitalist will be obliged to give the same wages to men alone, which they now give to men, women and children. . . . [Labourers must] prevent their wives and children from competing with them in the market, and beating down the price of labor.[11]

Seventy-five years later, an Independent Labour Party pamphlet affirmed that authentic freedom for women derived from not having to earn "any wage under any conditions."[12] Crowded labor markets made it impossible for working families to gain anything by sending another member into the wage force.[13]

In a pamphlet prepared for the Fabian Society, the radical Chiozza Money affirmed that "there is only one proper sphere of work for the married woman and that is her own home."[14] As two early historians of the British labor movement explained:

> The Trade Unions, whatever the faults in their economics or the lacunae in their reasoning, have never fallen into the blank and unfruitful individualism that has blighted the women's movement in the middle class; and the working woman we would submit has a far better chance to work out her economic salvation through solidarity and co-operation with her own class than by adopting the tactics and submitting to the tutelage of middle- or upper-class organizations.[15]

Ivy Pinchbeck, another early historian of working women, reached the same conclusion, arguing that "it was not always a sound economic proposition for the woman to be a wage earner." Women's earnings rarely compensated for the real value of lost domestic activities, they were subject to special forms of exploitation, and their earnings "only served to keep their husband's wages at the level of individual subsistence."[16]

Labor voices in the United States made similar claims for family justice and integrity. As the Philadelphia Trade Union warned its members:

> Oppose [the employment of women] with all your mind and with all your strength for it will prove our ruin. We must strive to obtain sufficient remuneration for our labor to keep the wives and daughters and sis-

ters of our people at home. . . . That cormorant capital will have every man, woman and child to toil; but let us exert our families to oppose its designs.[17]

Feminist Complaints

As the family-wage model gained intellectual and political support, feminist writers rose in dissent. The late nineteenth century radical Ada Nield Chew offered one set of arguments, maintaining that "babies and . . . domestic jobs are the chains which bind [employed wives]" and that "the line of progress is for married women to insist on . . . the right to paid work, and to refuse to perform domestic jobs simply because they are wives."[18] In a few scattered cases, such as the Lancashire women cotton workers of the mid- and late nineteenth century, women constructed social and economic environments premised on their primary labor.[19]

Later feminist voices, though, confessed to bewilderment over the family-wage concept: "Attacking the family wage is a bit like an atheist attacking god the father: She wants to say that it does not exist, that the false belief that it does has evil consequences and that even if it did exist it would not be a good thing."[20] In an attempt to put this issue to rest, some feminist historians have tried to explain the family wage as a betrayal of labor's interests. Rather than drawing all women into the work force, as predicted by Engels, Marx, and Kautsky, "capital" created a radical separation between home and workplace, they argue. Consequently, while men were oppressed by *having to do* wage work, women were oppressed by *not having to do* wage work: "the housewife emerged, alongside the proletarian [as] the two characteristic laborers of developed capitalist society."[21]

Heidi Hartmann has criticized this view of dual oppression for hopelessly romanticizing the preindustrial family. In her opinion, patriarchy has rested "most fundamentally in men's control over women's labor power." Capitalism and patriarchy, while independent forces, came to coexist in the late nineteenth century through the mechanism of the family wage. Men in the laboring classes procured women for them to dominate, to rear their children, and to provide "bodies for sex." Meanwhile, men in the capitalist class obtained a cadre of housewives who "produced and maintained healthier workers," secured better educations for and obedience from their children, and served as willing consumers of factory-produced goods. In sum, "[t]he family wage cemented the partnership between patriarchy and capital."[22]

Some recent writers have also cast the emerging welfare state as an ally of the family-wage regime. Mimi Abramovitz has suggested that American welfare policies were constructed so as to ensure the subordination of women throughout the social structure.[23] Zillah Eisenstein has argued that through the welfare state "the capitalist class . . . goes beyond capitalism in terms of representing and protecting the patriarchal and racist aspects of life."[24] Its desire to preserve the nuclear family "reflects its commitment to a division of labor that not only secures the greatest profit but also hierarchically orders the society culturally and politically."[25]

So goes the theory. But did capitalist leaders, in fact, enter into a patriarchal conspiracy with male labor? Except under union pressure, rarely. There are *no* significant examples of nineteenth- or early-twentieth-century British firms paying a family wage to male workers, in the absence of labor activism. In the United States, the exception proving the rule was Henry Ford. In 1914, he startled observers by announcing that he was immediately *doubling* the minimum rate paid to male autoworkers who were married "and taking good care of their families."[26]

But few of Ford's fellow industrialists followed suit, and one can argue that his initiative rested mainly on his desire to keep a nonunion shop. Indeed, between 1903 and 1930, the National Association of Manufacturers (NAM)—representing the larger American industrial corporations—waged a consistent campaign to expand every category of labor available, including women both married and single, children, and immigrants. Instead of cutting a "patriarchal deal" to lock women at home, the NAM passed in 1903 a resolution asserting that "no limitation should be placed upon the opportunities of any person to learn any trade to which he *or she* may be adapted." In a 1925 address, the NAM president ridiculed the mythical union striker who "felt that the returns from his efforts would not enable him to support his family in the style to which they were accustomed. And while the records don't say, he undoubtedly had a *large* family."[27]

Meanwhile, the association consistently fought against work rules placing special restrictions on, or protections over, working women. It also both sought and praised the U.S. Supreme Court's overturning of child-labor laws in 1918 and 1922.[28] There were even rumors circulating within progressive and trade-union circles that the NAM covertly funded the National Woman's Party, the architect of the Equal Rights Amendment and a regular advocate for equal work and pay for women.[29] In fact, the family-wage ideal might be accurately labelled as among the compensation principles which the NAM most fervently opposed.

There was no "patriarchal deal" resting on the family wage. While it was clearly part of the ideological repertoire of labor unions and progressive reformers in the academy and social work,[30] the family wage generally met scorn among the captains of industry. The principal thrust of nineteenth- and early-twentieth-century industrial capitalism remained liberal and individualistic. The real evidence is compelling that the working class "escaped the disciplinary power of the market only because it has resisted that power."[31] It was labor militancy and advocacy, not the beneficence or machinations of "capital," that primarily lay behind the campaign to build a family wage.

These efforts to construct a family-wage regime opposed the inherent tendencies of industrial capitalism to subordinate all social relationships to monetary exchanges and all human activity to the test of efficiency. As Alice Kessler-Harris has summarized: "In the labor market, enormous efforts had to be made to maintain boundaries that defied the immediate economic self-interest of employers and female employees and arguably, at least, of male workers in their capacity as husbands and fathers as well."[32] The family-wage concept combined the legacy of medieval "just price" theory with the vision of household economic independence as a necessary buttress for human autonomy. It also subordinated the free market in labor to local and cultural notions of justice, where the "breadwinner" role was related to the family and to the life cycle of individuals, and where men and women contributed to the sustenance of households in different ways. It affirmed that a wage system may have a social component that defies pure "supply and demand," and defines "the place of individuals relative to one another in the work community, in the neighborhood, and in the family."[33]

These efforts to build a family-wage system also challenged the expansive interests of the state. Analysts have shown that the modern welfare system is not an adjunct to a family-wage regime, but rather a substitute for it. A family wage fixed the redistribution of market income *within* families, where the employed laborer traded cash income for the noncash social labor of spouse and children. The welfare state, in contrast, represented the socialization of both parts of this exchange, through the taxation of earned income and the provision of state services to replace family functions. Carol Pateman has shown how women's growing dependence on the state was both a logical corollary to feminist goals and a stimulus to state entitlements as a substitute for family labor.[34] Frances Fox Piven has stressed the "large and important relationship" of women to the welfare state, reporting that 70 percent of government social-welfare jobs in the late twentieth century were held by women.[35]

The Family Wage, in Fact

In another attempt to dismiss the family wage, some feminist writers have argued that a true family-wage system never existed.[36] Yet the evidence is compelling that this ideal dominated labor goals throughout the North Atlantic region from the mid-nineteenth through the mid-twentieth centuries and that it had measurable effects on wages and the labor market. Looking at Belgium, one historian has identified a "thorough transformation" in the family life of workers between 1853 and 1891, based on a withdrawal of married women from the labor market and a dramatic rise in the real incomes of men.[37] Another investigation found that a family wage supported most Norwegian households from the late 1930s to the early 1970s.[38] The family-wage system clearly underpinned British trade-union political initiatives from 1842 to 1914.[39] The most recent income study of that nation and period found "that fairly substantial gains in material standards were achieved over the course of industrialization by the British working class," which was accompanied by the movement of women from wage-earning to domestic pursuits.[40]

In the United States, by the turn of the century the family-wage ideal extended well beyond union rhetoric. In the three thousand formal investigations of household income conducted between 1890 and the early 1930s, the focus shifted over time from the economic contribution of all family members to an emphasis on the male's family wage.[41] During the same years the American Federation of Labor embraced 75 to 80 percent of all unionized workers. Viewing the organization of women workers as "a hopeless endeavor," these craft unions agitated in contract settlements for the payment of a family wage.[42]

The family-wage concept survived the New Deal years. As Barbara Armstrong, an architect of the Social Security system, wrote: "There can be no dispute that it is today assumed that a male worker's wage should be a family wage rather than an individual wage. Indeed, such an assumption is the cornerstone of our social organization with its family unit."[43] As late as 1965, in a formal report to the International Labor Organization, the U.S. government affirmed "the basic legal principle which places on the husband the primary responsibility for support of his wife and family with secondary liability devolving on the wife."[44]

A dramatic change in the structure of the American family wage occurred in the early 1940s. Prior to then, the system rested primarily on legal barriers and forms of direct wage discrimination against categories of female workers. Marriage bans were common, as were labor laws requiring the special treatment of women, which discouraged their employment.[45]

The entry of the United States into World War II brought an end to direct wage discrimination. In February 1942, the National War Production Board proclaimed the "immediate extension" of industrial defense training for women on a basis of equality with men. The following November, the National War Labor Board (NWLB) issued General Order 16, which allowed defense contractors to increase wages for women who were being paid less than men "for comparable quality and quantity of work on the same or similar operations." By early 1944, over two thousand employers reported having made such adjustments, suggesting both the extent of direct discrimination before Pearl Harbor and the consequences of the war. A November 1945 NWLB ruling urged adopting of "the principle of a single evaluation line for all jobs in a plant regardless of whether the jobs are performed by men or women." Where only 13 percent of U.S. firms used this technique in 1939, 57 percent did so by 1947.[46]

Thus, by the late 1940s a family wage based on direct wage discrimination in favor of men within individual firms was becoming rare. One study of wages in the 1950s found no evidence "that employer discrimination is a major direct influence upon male-female differentials in average hourly earnings."[47] The proportion of adult women with earned incomes grew from 39 percent in 1947 to 61 percent in 1966.

Despite these developments, the wage gap between women and men actually grew. In 1939, median female earnings were 59.29 percent of males; by 1966, the figure had fallen to 53.66. Although direct wage discrimination against women had nearly vanished, a second and more powerful factor had more than compensated for this change: job segregation by gender, or the cultural recognition of "male" and "female" tasks. Victor Fuchs, using 1959–60 data, concluded that *most* of the forty percentage points difference between male and female average hourly earnings could be explained by the different employment roles ascribed to women and men.[48] Data from the U.S. Census Bureau showed that of the more than 250 distinct occupations listed, half of all employed women were clustered in only twenty-one of them, while half of all men crowded into sixty-five occupations.[49]

Vernon Clover has offered a detailed analysis of the structure of the labor market in the 1945–65 period. While he noted that a slightly lower proportion of employed women worked full time in 1965 compared to 1950, the primary cause of the widening wage gap was the crowding of women into employment categories that were over 90 percent female, including file clerks, keypunch operators, secretaries, stenographers, and typists. Meanwhile, women lost ground in occupational groups that were over 95 percent male, such as attorneys, auditors, chemists, engineers, and draftsmen. Not by coincidence, of the thirteen occupational groups surveyed, clerical workers enjoyed the *smallest* increase in average salary during the 1950s, while chemists and chief accountants recorded the highest. As Clover concluded, "the traditional social taboos against females in certain kinds of occupations and levels of responsibility are evidently stronger than is commonly realized."[50]

It is possible to construct an estimation of the family wage in the United States for the second half of the twentieth century, using data on the income of married couple households provided by the U.S. Census Bureau and calculating the ratio of those with wives in the labor force over those with wives not employed:

$$R_F = I_2 / I_1$$

(R_F = Family Wage Ratio; I_2 = Median Family Income, Wife in Paid Labor Force; I_1 = Median Family Income, Wife Not in Paid Labor Force)

This simple ratio proves sensitive to a variety of aggregated factors: the impact of job segregation on household income; the relative degree of career commitment by men and women; the effects of protective legislation; the influence of seniority; and the relative use of part-time work. In a pure "family-wage economy," this ratio would tend toward (but never reach) 1.00, as law and custom reinforced a substantially higher net wage for the male breadwinner and marginal compensation for the married woman. In an economy of pure gender equality, this ratio would tend toward 2.0, as the man and the woman in the average marriage approached complete market equality, and the one-income couple was progressively disadvantaged. The trend of this ratio for the United States between 1951 and 2003 is presented in Graph A.

These results show a relatively stable ratio between 1951 and 1969, varying in a narrow range between 1.25 and 1.31, reaching the lower figure in both 1958 and 1960. The period from

GRAPH A

U.S. Family Wage Ratio = $\dfrac{\text{Median Family Income, Wife in Paid Labor Force}}{\text{Median Family Income, Wife Not in Paid Labor Force}}$

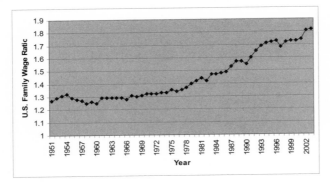

1970 to 1982 reveals a fairly steady rise in the ratio from 1.31 to 1.42. Thereafter, the increase accelerates, reaching 1.73 in 2000 and leaping to 1.82 three years later. It is safe to conclude that a fairly strong and stable family-wage economy, clearly evident in the 1950s and existing as late as 1969, had disappeared by the early twenty-first century.

What caused this rapid change? To begin with, the historic opposition of labor unions to wage equality, still evident in the early 1960s, had collapsed not ten years later. While the Equal Pay Act of 1963 enjoyed formal labor support, the proposed Equal Rights Amendment [ERA] to the U.S. Constitution—with its feminist-industrialist pedigree dating from the 1920s—continued to draw scorn from union leaders. They saw the ERA as a direct legal threat to the mix of seniority, apprenticeship, and wage preferences for the male worker. By 1968, however, the United Auto Workers (UAW) played an instrumental role in founding the National Organization for Women and pledged to take action "to bring women into full partnership in the mainstream of American society now, exercising all of the privileges and responsibilities thereof in truly equal partnership with men."[51] As late as 1972, the AFL-CIO continued to oppose the ERA. The next year, after stormy debate, the organization endorsed the amendment as "a symbol of commitment to equal opportunity for women and equal status for women." With this action, the 150-year-long effort by American labor unions to create and defend a family-wage economy came to an end.[52]

A second cause of the disappearance of a family wage resting on job segregation by gender was the addition of the word *sex* to Title VII of the Civil Rights Act of 1964. As originally proposed by the Lyndon B. Johnson administration, this portion of the act would have prohibited employers from segregating or classifying employees, for any purpose, on the basis of race, color, religion, or national origin. Yet during floor debate in the U.S. House of Representatives, "Dixiecrat" Howard Smith of Virginia proposed an amendment to the bill adding the word *sex* to the list of prohibited discriminations. While his purpose was unclear and probably malicious (virtually all Democrats favoring racial segregation supported the measure),[53] the measure won approval after cursory discussion on a 168 to 133 vote. The House amendment survived a conference with the Senate, which also never really debated the issue or purpose of placing *sex* in Title VII, and this change became law.

For a few years, the impact of the measure was uncertain. Then in 1967, President Johnson issued Executive Order 11375, which prohibited federal contractors from discrimination in employment on the basis of sex and mandated "affirmative," "result-oriented" measures to eliminate job segregation by gender. Between 1968 and 1971, the Equal Employment Opportunities Commission [EEOC] "converted Title VII into a magna carta for female workers, grafting to it a set of rules and regulations that certainly could not have passed Congress in 1964, and perhaps not a decade later, either."[54] In 1969, the EEOC struck down all state laws giving special protection to women, arguing that they had "ceased to be relevant to our technology or to the expanding role of the female worker in our economy."[55] EEOC rulings on sex-specific hiring directly undermined the practice of job segregation by gender. The effect was huge. One analyst suggested that in the absence of enforcement of Title VII, "the male/female earnings gap would not have remained constant, but *would have increased, between 1967 and 1974.*" Instead, EEOC efforts directly narrowed the male-female earnings differential during these years by 14 percent in the private sector, by 2 percent in the governmental sector, and by 7 percent in the economy as a whole.[56] Another analyst calculated a narrowing of the "gender gap" in income from .617 in 1971 to .700 in 1987.[57]

Equal Wages and Family Decline

Several consequences followed from this dramatic weakening of the family wage. First, family households with only a single male wage-earner experienced a *decline* in real income, a predictable result of the effective expansion in the labor supply achieved through the elimination of gender barriers. Using constant [1993] dollars, the median income of married-couple families, when the wife was *not* in the paid labor force, was $34,956 in 1973 and $30,218 in 1993, a decline of 13.6 percent.[58]

Second, the "terms of trade" turned against single-earner families. Relative to housing, for example, the ratio:

$$R = \frac{\text{Median Price Paid for New Single Family House}}{\text{Median Annual Family Income (married couples)}}$$

climbed from 2.52 in 1970 to 4.13 in 1988 for families with the wife not in the paid labor force, a 64 percent increase. For families with working wives, this ratio climbed from 1.91 in 1970 to 2.63 in 1988, only a 38 percent increase.[59] Similar shifts in the terms of trade might be plotted relative to the purchase of automobiles and major appliances. Simply put, single-income families found themselves at a mounting competitive disadvantage, relative to two-income families, in the acquisition of consumer goods.

Third, these changes led to the declining well-being of children. Work by the Annie Casey Foundation has shown the close relationship between the rise in the percentage of men ages 25 to 34 earning less than a "poverty line" wage (from 13 percent in 1969 to 32 percent in 1993) and the increased percentage of children living in female-headed households (from 11 to 23 percent over the same years).[60] On the other hand, families with the wife not in the labor force (numbering 21,534,000 in 1991) were both *more likely* to have dependent children at home and were, on average, *larger* than families where the mother was in the full-time paid labor force. Both factors were related to poverty status.

Consequently, this era's nagging problem of American children living below the poverty line derived not only from the rising proportion of children in female-headed households, but also from the number of children living in intact, two-parent families with only one earner. Between 1980 and 1991, for example, the real income of married couple families with the husband as the sole earner declined by 6 percent, while the real income of married, two-earner families rose by 5 percent. Over the same period, the proportion of married couple families with children below the poverty level climbed by 10 percent. In 1992, 9.1 percent of these families earned less than $10,000. By comparison, only 1.8 percent of married-couple families with the wife in the labor force had incomes below this figure.

The fourth consequence of the disappearance of the family-wage system was that American families became fully industrialized or commodified for the first time. As married women with children moved into the labor market there was a sharp decline in "the production of immediate use values within the family." Gardening, food preparation, home repairs, child care, and other residual forms of home production surrendered to market-provided services, meaning that "the material basis of the individual family [was] disappearing in the sphere of consumption, as it had previously in the sphere of production."[61] Indeed, "the universalization of wage labor" lay behind this era's expansion of the service sector, the accelerated decline of the family as an autonomous economic unit, and the disappearance of other forms of social labor more compatible with family bonds.[62]

In short, the nearly complete industrialization of social life and the progressive loss of family functions and autonomy were two aspects of the same late-twentieth-century phenomenon. With its economic rationale sharply reduced, the family based on marriage was displaced by rampant divorce, a rising number of out-of-wedlock births, declining marriage rates, later marriages, and more permanent singlehood and cohabitation.

The linkage of these changes to the decline of the family-wage system can be gauged through two relatively sensitive measures of family commitment: *the marriage rate* and *the marital fertility rate*. Graph B shows a significant connection between the decline of the family-wage system and a growing avoidance of marriage. Graph C traces the relationship between shifts in the family wage and marital fertility; it reveals a significant bond particularly strong during the years 1951–72 and continuing in weaker form as late as 1987. (After that year, the relationship failed, suggesting that the decline in marital fertility had reached a plateau.) In both eras, though, the Family-Wage Index rose as the marriage rate and the marital fertility rate declined.

By the close of the twentieth century there was mounting evidence of family decay. Without the protection to family autonomy afforded by the family-wage system, family households were failing to form or were left as loosely organized entities of relatively minor social and economic significance.

GRAPH B

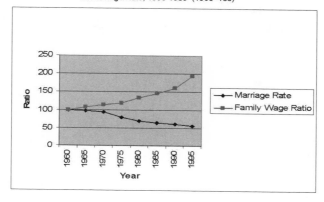

Change in Family Wage Ratio Compared
to Marriage Rate, 1960-1985 (1960=100)

GRAPH C

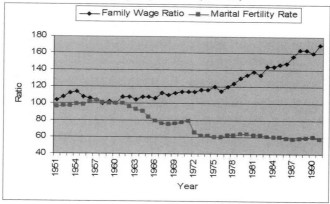

Change in Family Wage Ratio Compared
to Fertility Rate, 1951-1991 (1960=100)

As Christopher Lasch has suggested, the late twentieth century did not witness the strengthening of patriarchy and a family wage, but rather the mutually reinforcing expansion of corporate capitalism and the centralizing state, which occurred largely at the expense of the family. As family households weakened, both the state apparatus and the corporate structure grew stronger. The result, according to Lasch, was not greater per-

sonal independence. Rather, under a regime of state capitalism, both women and men faced new forms of servitude: to an
impersonal state bureaucracy; and to "the regressive psychology
of industrialism, which reduces the citizen to a consumer and
bombards him with images of immediate and total gratifica-
tion."[63]

The historical record reviewed here sustains the argument
that, in order to survive as a meaningful center of autonomy,
the family needs an economic base. By limiting the intrusions
of corporations (via wages) and the state (via taxes) into the
household economy, the family-wage system constructed and
sustained between 1830 and the late 1960s performed, however
imperfectly, such a task. By century's end, however, rehabilitation of the family-wage regime was impossible. The sustaining
cultural assumptions behind purposeful gender discrimination
no longer existed. Nor did organized labor support. Moreover,
the narrow, constricted role of "the homemaker" developed in
the late nineteenth century and institutionalized through the
"home economics" movement proved unsustainable. Homemaking as a twentieth-century profession never gained a true
sense of craftsmanship. In many respects, it simply accelerated
the submission of the family to industrialization and consumer-
ism.[64]

All the same, the sociological, psychological, and crimino-
logical evidence from that era shows that intact families based
on marriage were superior as nurturers of the young and as
positive factors in adult well-being. Children reared in such
settings were significantly less likely to be victims of abuse,[65]
to attempt suicide,[66] to use illegal drugs,[67] and to commit other
criminal acts.[68] Children raised in intact, married-couple families were healthier in mind and body than children raised in
other settings[69] and more likely to succeed in school.[70] Married
adults were also healthier and much less inclined to commit
suicide than their divorced or never-married peers.[71]

On Children and Liberty

Given this record, two historic justifications for the family wage deserve additional attention. The first is the needs of children, and the second is the role played by the family wage in forestalling the full industrialization of families.

Wherever it has spread, the industrial process has shattered the direct linkage of work and home. Under its domain, most adults came to labor and sleep in different places, a radical change in human history. As factory-produced goods displaced those once made within households, the new labor market also took form in centralized plants and offices. The critical questions became: Who shall care for the children? How shall incomes, earned by sole workers, be adjusted to meet the greater needs of households with offspring?

Australia was the first nation to attempt systematic policy answers to these questions. As a recent historical survey has shown, the dissociation of paid labor from the home sharply reduced the ability of Australian women to supplement the earnings of poorly paid husbands. Out of necessity, these households turned to an enhanced sexual division of labor within the nuclear family, to creation of the "breadwinner" and the "homemaker" as—in one progressive historian's words—"a buffer against the most obvious forms of capitalist exploitation."[72]

Families also turned to political action. Responding to reports of the "scandalous" treatment of employed women and children, the state parliament of Victoria approved the "Factories and Shops Act of 1896." This measure created elective boards in six industries with the power to set minimum rates, which were fixed to a "living family wage" standard. The Australian system rested on a "discrediting of the principle of equal pay for equal work" in favor of pay linked to actual or potential family responsibilities. Over time, the wage courts settled on an "individual" female wage that was 54 percent of that paid to men (a figure astonishingly close to the 53.66 percent found in the U.S.A. in 1966, perhaps suggesting a "natural" level for this figure).[73]

Boards of this type soon appeared in Britain. The minimum wage movement in the United States also built directly on the Australian experiment. Between 1912 and 1923, a dozen U.S. states with progressive majorities (including Massachusetts, Wisconsin, and California) established wage commissions and subordinate industry boards to fix minimum rates. All of these laws aimed at the protection of family relationships and children, and all calculated the female minimum wage on an "individual" rather than a family basis. This, it was hoped, "would exclude from industry that great body of inexperienced temporary women workers who are partly supported from sources other than their wages, and who, therefore, *demoralize* the entire wage system."[74]

In 1923, a Republican-dominated U.S. Supreme Court struck down these state-level minimum wage laws, with the justices ruling that differences between men and women "have now come almost, if not quite, to the vanishing point," and that therefore there was no longer any way to justify the regulation of wages based on gender.[75] Critics lodged other complaints against a state-coerced minimum "family wage." They argued that since few families had exactly three dependent children at any given time, a "family of five" standard conjured up a vast horde of "fictitious children" needing support: two million in Australia; sixteen million in Britain; and forty-eight million in the United States. Truly needy families with four or more children received an underpayment for male labor, while bachelors were grossly overpaid for their work. Meanwhile, between 20 and 40 percent of women workers who were partly or wholly responsible for youthful dependents struggled to raise their children on an "individual" wage.

These critics concluded that such inefficiencies justified an alternative approach: the creation of a child's endowment to provide an income floor for households with children. Minimum wages, fixed by law, should be sufficient for the support of one, or perhaps two, persons, while the child endowment would pay a cash allowance for each dependent child, together with an allowance for the mother in recognition of her labor and need for maintenance. Eleanor Rathbone, writing in England,[76] and Paul Douglas, writing in the United States,[77] acknowledged the possibility of using voluntary industrial funds for this purpose. Yet both authors preferred the creation of a state child endowment, funded by employer or payroll taxes, as a more efficient and universal vehicle for redistribution.

The second historical justification for the family wage was broader in its implications and incapable of resolution through a child endowment or allowance system. It held that *the family wage was necessary to protect families and their members from full industrialization, or immersion into state capitalism.*

Late-twentieth-century "proletarianization" could be defined as the gradual elimination of independent sources of household income other than wages and the "redistributed" wages of state transfers, where economic gains from private property, "commons" rights, informal economic activity, household production, and other forms of nonmarket work were steadily displaced by factory labor, commercially purchased goods, and public welfare. Most working-class families in the nineteenth and early twentieth centuries struggled to avoid this end. In a compelling article, Jane Humphries has shown how the effort by rural laborers in England to hold on to "commons" rights to grazing plots and woodlands in the face of legally mandated "enclosures" rested on the desire to preserve some sense of liberty. Access to a "commons" meant that a wageless laborer "would not starve. Nor would his family." The commons also liberated landless workers from the beck and call of the emerging industrial farmers. "In the terms of the times these were not paltry degrees of freedom," writes Humphries.[78] In those places where the full industrialization of social relations broke through, the result was the elimination of an economic base to the family, very low fertility, and full dependence on employers for subsistence.[79]

Under a family-wage regime, the working family accepted the industrialization of one of its members as a necessary adaptation to the new order. However, the value of the domestic labor of others in the family was retained by the family itself, in defiance of industrial capitalism's incentives. Most workers also exhibited a distrust of state solutions to the negative consequences of industrialism. Under conditions of full industrialization, they understood that family autonomy would be surrendered in exchange for benefits dependent on an elusive control of the political process. Workers also perceived that the more likely prospect was an alliance between political rulers and employers, to the detriment of labor: something like Hilaire Belloc's Servile State. Working-class women, for example, distrusted intervention by agents of welfare capitalism, fearing the effects of state benefits on their husbands' incentives to work, and on their own pivotal position in the family.[80] From a material perspective, the nonlaboring members of the working class reasoned that their welfare could be better secured through informal arrangements, rather than through modern, state-controlled channels.[81]

They also preferred that the dependency problem still be resolved, in large part, within the family. Besides the care of children, every human society faces a second "dependency" challenge. Who shall provide for those adults unable to care for themselves, the sick, the handicapped, and the very old? Payment of a family wage meant that kinship could continue to mediate this altruistic community function, securing for nonworking adults a fair portion of the remuneration for workers. As Humphries puts it, "[t]he battle for a 'family wage' was [a] . . . demonstration of working class insistence on the integrity of their own kinship structures."[82]

The Power of Home Production

The family wage also granted validity and integrity to other forms of labor, including household or family production. While industrial capitalism has a clear tendency toward the universal extension of the sphere of wage labor, other forms of work can and perhaps *must* survive in order to preserve the basis of social life.[83] In their provocative analysis of "women's claims," Lisa Peattie and Martin Rein have rejected the dominant position given to wage income by both Marxist and liberal analysts. They have urged equal attention to family claims rooted in notions of solidarity and interdependence. For most women, they have noted, family-centered work has been the most important form of labor, giving credence to the otherwise inexplicable preference shown by many women for the family-wage regime.[84]

Industrial capitalism certainly obscured the value of household production. In the early nineteenth century, commons rights and various types of cottage industries allowed mothers and wives to increase their real family income without becoming industrial wage workers or disrupting child care. By the end of that century, however, the still substantial contribution of women's household production to family support was being either veiled or denied. As Jane Humphries has explained, capitalist relations both "corrupt pre-industrial family relations" and simultaneously hide "the primitively communal core which the family retains in the union of labouring and non-labouring individuals."[85] Only recently have economists fairly documented the worth of this hidden "nonindustrial" labor. Reuben Gronau has calculated the average value of home production of American wives, near the end of the American family wage regime, to have exceeded 70 percent of the family's after-tax income.[86] With at least one young child in the home, this unpaid, untaxed contribution was nearly *equal* to potential market earnings.[87]

Using data from the same period, Scott Burns estimated the value of household labor to be 50 percent of all formal labor income in the U.S.[88]

The incentives within a family wage structure encouraged the existence and strengthening of this partially hidden home economy. Families were able to defend their standard of living and their autonomy by restricting the entry of their members into the industrialized sector, by demanding a family-sustaining wage for the one family member in the formal labor market, by keeping a wary distance from the economic and political elites of a state capitalist order, and by appropriating in full the real gains of household production. With the disappearance of the family wage regime, circa 1970, families faced social, economic, and political perils that were at once both old and very new.

3

Alexander Chayanov and the Theory of Peasant Utopia

One of the great human tragedies of the disaster-ridden twentieth century was the destruction of the Russian and Ukrainian peasantries. In the whole Russian Empire of 1910, there were 135 million peasants (out of a total population of 158 million). In European Russia alone, 93 million peasants formed 84 percent of the population. These were not the brutish knuckle-draggers of caricature. For decades this great mass of family farmers had grown more self-aware. Romantic Slavophilism of the 1840s stressed the peasant virtues of the countryside. Emancipation of the serfs in 1861 led to the creation of *zemstvos*, local peasant councils involving a form of rural democracy. The Populist Movement launched in the 1880s brought Russian intellectuals into the countryside, eager "to go to the people" and reconnect with nature. Peasant unrest in 1905 helped shepherd in a quasi-democratic national parliament. Then came the slaughter and

privations of the Great War, the Bolshevik Revolution, the violence surrounding "war communism," frequent purges, "de-
Kulakization," forced collectivization, and the vast disruptions
of the Second World War. By 1945, as many as 40 million of
the peasants were dead; the remainder had been forced off their
land, many into the gulag, their way of life pulverized.

This historical sketch poses intriguing questions. In the absence of this cycle of violence, had there been relative peace,
how would the Russian peasantry have evolved? What would
this vast peasant majority have made out of a Russia experimenting with democracy and rapidly entering the industrial
age?

One answer comes from the pen of the Russian economist
Alexander V. Chayanov, who wrote under the pseudonym Ivan
Kremnev. Published in 1920 and titled *The Journal of My Brother
Alexei to the Land of Peasant Utopia*, his book presents a decentralized, oddly progressive, democratic Russian peasant state
set in 1984.[1] This novella has a wonderfully light side to it.
For example, its protagonist, Alexei Kremnev, wakes up after
travelling through time and asks: "Have I really become the
hero of a Utopian novel? . . . A pretty stupid situation." It turns
out that the great national sport of Peasant Utopia in 1984 is
"Knucklebones," an ancient form of jacks followed with all the
intensity of the real future's World Cup soccer. And on meeting his hostess in the future, Alexei grows enchanted with "this
Utopian woman, . . . her almost classical head, perfectly set on
a strong neck, her broad shoulders and full breasts, which raised
her shirt collar with every breath." When her sister proves even
more alluring, the novelist writes: "Alexei was positively crazy
about Utopian women."[2]

However, this novella was also a serious effort to portray
during Russia's early Communist era a noncommunist alternative also committed to equality and social justice. It is a plea to
avoid the disasters looming within a socialized economy by in-

stead defending and encouraging a nation of free peasants. The utopian novella is grounded in Chayanov's rich and original economic thought, outlined most completely in *Peasant Farm Organization*, published in 1923.

Back to the Future

The Journey of My Brother Alexei to the Land of Peasant Utopia opens with a curious "forward" by P. Orlovskii, the pseudonym of V. V. Vorovskii, a publicist and professional diplomat. Perhaps because the novella is "a scarcely veiled criticism of the narrow, somewhat joyless Bolshevik reality of 1920,"[3] Vorovskii goes out of his way to stress the unreality of Chayanov's utopia, even trying to turn it into a negative dystopia. He acknowledges that the volume is another attempt to show "those ideal conditions" in which "all the contradictions and injustices of a capitalist society" would be resolved. However, he says, the story also emphasizes the "self-exploitation" of the "petty proprietor," the "complete enslavement of man by the soil." Ignoring the law of diminishing returns, the "ideologists of the petty land-owning peasantry," such as the author Kremnev, "want to preserve the peasant farm at all costs." To do so, they retain certain aspects of capitalism, including an exchange economy and monetary circulation. This "reactionary" utopia would work, Vorovskii continues, only by protecting Russian grain and artisan production behind massive tariffs. Having the "petty peasantry" in office would also mean "the ruin of towns." Indeed, "[t]o imagine that social equality and social justice can be preserved while preserving the individual farm, and, in industry, even capitalist production . . . is to understand nothing of the laws of development of contemporary societies."[4]

This negative spin, however, fails to harm Chayanov's essentially positive portrait of the land of Peasant Utopia. The story opens in autumn 1921 as Kremnev, a Bolshevik operative charged with eliminating the peasantry, leaves a meeting held in Moscow. He has just voted for a decree to destroy the family hearth. Phrases from the debate flash through his mind:

> By destroying the family hearth we are dealing the final blow to the bourgeois system!

> Our decree forbidding taking meals at home eliminates from our lives the joyful poison of the bourgeois family and firmly establishes the socialist principle forever.

> The cosiness of family life leads to possessiveness, the petty proprietor's joys conceal the seeds of capitalism.

Returning to his "half-destroyed family hearth fated in a week's time to be destroyed completely," he examines his shelf of utopian novels—including tomes by William Morris, Sir Thomas More, and Edward Bellamy—and mutters to them that "[y]our solitary dreams are now common beliefs, your greatest audacities have become an official programme . . . !" Then he pulls down a volume by the Russian populist Alexander Herzen. Freeing his mind from "the hypnosis of Soviet daily life, new, unhackneyed thoughts" stir within him. He reads that weak, puny, and stupid generations will soon be smothered by an eruption: "Then spring will come; young life will burgeon on their gravestones, . . . a wild, new power will burst forth in the youthful breast of the young nations." Alexei understands this to mean that socialism will grow to its "utmost limits, to absurdity," that "a cry of refusal" will then break out among the people, "and there will be once more a mortal struggle in which socialism, in the position of today's conservatism, will be defeated by another, unknown revolution still to come."

As he ponders what this "new rising" will be, an odor of sulphur fills the room; the hands of the clock disappear in a whirl; the walls grow distorted and tremble. He falls on a sofa and loses consciousness.

Alexei awakens to a new, radically different Moscow. Through a window he sees that the Kremlin is still there, but everything else is unfamiliar. Vast blocks of buildings are gone, replaced by "gardens everywhere" and "sprawling clumps of trees" woven together by boulevards with "streams of pedestrians, motor cars, and carriages" pouring through them "in a living river." Alexei examines the room. It is light and airy, with furniture made of red wood with green-yellow upholstery in a "strongly russified Babylonian style" revealing a "thirst for craftsmanship." He spots a newspaper in the room bearing the date "5 September 1984." He has jumped forward more than sixty years! Phrases leap from the page—"peasantry"; "the past era of urban culture"; "state collectivism of sad memory." These also suggest a very different world.

Alexei soon discovers that he has been mistaken for Charlie Mann, a visitor to Russia from America. He is in the care of the Minin family, a vast clan living next to each other on their family farms in houses "built in the simple style of the sixteenth century." A grey-haired patriarch, Alexei Alexandrovich Minin, is there to arrange for his tour and to answer his questions. The author concludes that "the family is the family, and ever shall be."[5]

Alexei also learns that during the 1920s, "the peasantry . . . proved hard to communize." The peasants steadily increased their representation in the Congress of Soviets, and by 1934 power was firmly in their hands. Having learned from the 1917 revolution of "the danger" to a democratic regime from "huge conglomerations of urban population," the peasants pushed through a decree abolishing towns with more than twenty thousand inhabitants. An urban revolt occurred in 1937, but it was put down and the Moscow streets emptied while "the city's skycrapers were destroyed by the hundreds." Alexei's host continues: "Now the whole area for hundreds of miles around Moscow is a continuous agricultural settlement, intersected by rectangles of common forest, strips of co-operative pastures and huge climatic parks." Married couples and their children hold allotments of eight to ten acres, with their houses set side-by-side along roads for dozens of miles. Township centers feature local schools, libraries, entertainment halls, and other community facilities.

The failure of socialism, one of the Minins explains, lay in its origin "in the dungeons of the German capitalist factories, nurtured in the minds of an urban proletariat haunted by forced labour." Wage-slaves themselves, the workers in constructing their own ideology made "servitude an article of faith of the future system; and created an economy in which all were performers and only a few individuals possessed the right to creative activity."[6] This had been Russian communism.

The patriarch Minin reports that the social principles of the modern peasant order were not new: "our task was to consolidate the old, centuries-old, principles on which from time immemorial the peasant economy had been based." He continues:

> Our economic system, like that of ancient Rus', is founded on the individual peasant farm. We considered it, and still do so, the ideal model of economic activity. In it, man confronts nature; in it, labour comes into creative contact with all the forces of the cosmos. . . . Every workman is a creator, each manifestation of his individuality represents the art of work.

Each family raises its own food supply on its acreage, using only simple tools. As a Minin brother tells Alexei: "Our harvests of more than three tons an acre are achieved by practically looking after each ear of grain individually. Agriculture has never been as manual as now."[7] The old man notes that living and working in the countryside is the healthiest way to live, with the most variety, adding "This is man's natural condition, from which he was exiled by the demon of capitalism."[8]

All the same, the Peasant Utopia retained—of necessity— some elements of the capitalist regime. Whereas "the pre-socialist world . . . was driven by the power of human greed, by hunger," the Communists put every worker on a state wage "and so removed all incentive from the work." After winning control, the peasants restored "all the mechanisms which stimulate private economic activity," such as piece rates, bonuses for managers, and premium prices for desired farm products. To spur on capital formation, they encouraged cooperatives to form "social capital funds," or credit unions.

Under pure capitalism, the family patriarch says, industry had assumed "a pathological, monstrous condition." All the same, in most branches of production a return to artisan activity or cottage industry was deemed impractical. Instead, Peasant Utopia turned to cooperative enterprises with guaranteed large markets, which "nipped in the bud any chance of competition for most products." Heavy taxes on capitalist factories aided the process:

> However, we still have private initiative of [the] capitalist type; in those areas where collectively managed enterprises are ineffective, and in those cases where an organizing genius can overcome, thanks to advanced technology, the effects of our Draconian taxation.

Indeed, this retention of a sphere for entrepreneurship had another motive: "to preserve for our comrade co-operators a degree of threat from . . . competition, and thus save them from technical stagnation." For even though "our present-day capitalists, too, have shark-like propensities, . . . we all know that there are sharks in the sea so that the other fish should not doze."[9]

Society and the state are no idols in the land of Peasant Utopia: "We are particularly cautious about the state, which we use only when necessity dictates." As a *faux* editorial in the 1984 paper *The Sign of the Zodiac* explains: "The great decree . . . on the citizen's inalienable rights made the state into an obedient instrument of human individuality and destroyed the fetish of its sovereign rights." As patriarch Minin adds: "we have stripped the state of virtually all social and economic functions, and the ordinary man has hardly any contact with it." Government, such as it was, came through a system of local peasant councils. Peasant Utopia made every effort to push responsibilities and tasks ever closer to these councils. Moreover, nine-tenths of the needed work was done outside government: "various societies, co-operatives, congresses, leagues, newspapers, other organs of public opinion, academies and, finally, clubs—that is the social fabric which constitutes the life of the nation." Again from *The Sign of the Zodiac*: "Our problems do not require the thunderbolts of state power, but can be more easily and more firmly resolved by means of voluntary social construction."[10] This reliance on civil society allows "a freedom from authority."

The Minin family explains to Alexei how the founders of Peasant Utopia were troubled by one thought: "are the higher forms of culture possible with a population scattered in the countryside?" To shape a positive answer, they moved the theaters, the museums, the people's universities, the choral societies, and sporting activities into the country. A law of obligatory travel, borrowed from the medieval guilds, required young men and women to see the world and expand their horizons. A two-year conscription for military and labour service brought moral discipline: "[s]ports, rhythmic gymnastics, eurythmics, factory work, marches, manoevres, navvying—all this helps to mould our citizens." As a result, the number of those who drink "at the fountain-head of culture and life" steadily grows: "Nector and ambrosia have ceased to be the food of the Olympians alone, they now enrich the homes of humble villagers."[11] Peasant realism in art also now rules, with Pieter Brueghel as the acknowledged master. *The Sign of the Zodiac* reports that The Union of Peasant Choral Societies, with forty thousand singers from all thirty-two Great Russian provinces, will perform a certain Mazharov's new composition, "The Land Brings Forth Live Shoots," on May Day 1984. Historical studies, meanwhile, now focus on the stories of the common citizens—gleaned through their letters and diaries. As a book reviewer comments: "now we see before us the depths of national life, the true subsoil of history."[12]

In the end, Alexei's real identity is exposed. He spends a few days in a comfortable prison. Most of his fellow inmates are "anthroposophists"—that is, secular humanists "who had succumbed" to "the great German idea." Released from jail, he walks away alone, "friendless and penniless, to face life in a Utopian country he hardly knew."

The Peasants' Moral Economy

Animating this fanciful story was a provocative and dynamic microeconomics of the peasant or family farm. Rejecting both the neoclassical economics of Adam Smith and David Ricardo and the socialism of Karl Marx, Chayanov posited a scientifically grounded "moral economy"[13] that threatened the very existence of the Bolshevik regime in the Soviet Union and drew the particular ire of Joseph Stalin.

Who was Alexander Vasilevich Chayanov? Born in 1888, little is known about his early life. In 1909, at age twenty-one, he published his first essays on agricultural economics. A year later he received his Ph.D. from the Moscow Agrarian Institute, with his dissertation on *The Southern Limit of the Three-Course System of Peasant Fields at the Start of the Twentieth Century*. Other early publications focused on the role of "Agronomists Advising the Public" (1911) and "The Problem of Training Agricultural Officers" (1914). Although no Bolshevik, he was an active participant in the Russian Revolution of 1917. Two years later, Chayanov became director of the Institute of Agricultural Economy, a think tank at Moscow's Timiryazov Agricultural College. From 1919 to 1930, he was the Soviet Union's leading authority on agricultural economics. During the early 1920s, he served the central government as Deputy Minister of Agriculture.[14]

It was in these years that Chayanov inspired the "School for Analysis of Peasant Production and Organization," a neo-populist intellectual movement better known by the shorthand "Organization and Production School." His colleagues included A. N. Chelintsev, N. P. Makarov, A. A. Rybinkov, G. A. Stundenski, and A. N. Minin, some of whose surnames he borrowed for *Peasant Utopia*. Chayanov also worked with the great Russian macroeconomist N. D. Kondratiev, the theorist behind the Long Wave (which held that Western capitalist economies have fifty- to sixty-year cycles of prosperity followed by depression). Projects of the Organization and Production School included the development of a unique bookkeeping system for peasant farms and a detailed study of specialty crops and cottage crafts found in the countryside. The more this group studied the peasant economy, though, the more its members believed that existing economic theories did not apply in this sphere. In Chayanov's words, they needed "to construct a separate theory of the family undertaking working for itself."[15] The early 1920s offered them a political opportunity. After the disasters of "war communism," the Bolsheviks retreated on the economic front. Under the "New Economic Policy," they shelved schemes to collectivize peasant land-holdings and allowed "capitalists" to operate in industry on a modest scale: the very order outlined in *Peasant Utopia*. Russia's future economic life appeared to lie along the lines laid out by Chayanov and his team.[16]

With some justice, Chayanov insisted that he was no ideologue; rather, he was a scientist whose analysis rested on observation. Starting in the 1870s, the tsarist government had collected a vast array of statistics on peasant social and economic life. Already by 1910, agro-economists had found "that peasant economic behavior in the Russian countryside was not consistent with the simple allocation models of classical political economy." Notably, the peasants did not appear to maximize profits or recognize "marginal utility."[17] Chayanov based his alternate approach on a remarkably detailed 1910 investigation of 101 peasant households in Starobel'sk, with the results published in 1915. According to economic historian Teodor Shanin, these findings "empirically validated—or at least illustrated" Chayanov's general theory of peasant economy.[18]

The Austrian school of neoclassical liberal economics had a decided influence on Chayanov. He noted that he and his colleagues faced Communist critics who argued that "the Organization and Production School does not use [the] Marxist method and is, in essence, an offspring of the Austrian marginal utility school."[19] Austrian-school concepts, language, and logic do fill Chayanov's analysis; he confesses that terms "such as 'subjective evaluation,' 'marginal labor expenditure,' and even 'the utility of the worker's marginal *ruble* of earnings' are to be found in the works of the present author."[20] However, Chayanov distanced himself from the Austrians on a key point. He refused to extend a microeconomic "subjective evaluation of the utility of objects" to "an entire system of . . . national economy."[21]

Chayanov's theory of peasant economy must also be seen as part of a broader search for a "theory of family economy," a phrase used in the title of the 1923 German edition of his *Peasant Farm Organization*.[22] Chayanov proposes the concept of "the natural economy," where the unit of production is also the unit of consumption and where profits and wages play no role. Such a system prevails on what he calls "the fully natural family farm." He sees this "natural family economy" as one of four distinct economic types, the other three being capitalist, Communist, and slave.[23]

Chayanov stresses that the family economy found on peasant farms is "coincident" with other economic systems; that is, it can coexist with capitalism, slavery, or communism. These distinct, "closed" systems then "communicate with the others only by those objective economic elements they [have] had in common," conversations he outlines in a fascinating chart of economic systems. For example, capitalism and the "natural family economy" can share in "reproduction of the means of production" but have nothing to say to each other about interest, wages, or land rent.[24] Individuals placed in any of these systems find themselves adjusting to distinctive rules and incentives. As Chayanov comments regarding a well-known finance capitalist:

> It seems to us that if Rothschild were to flee to some agrarian country . . . and be obliged to engage in peasant labor, he would obey the rules of conduct established by the Organization and Production School, for all his bourgeois acquisitive psychology.[25]

Neither Ricardo Nor Marx

From these assumptions, Chayanov argues that neither the neoclassical economics of Smith and Ricardo nor Marxism applied to the great mass of Russians living on "natural family farms" circa 1920. As land-use economists R. Roberts and T. Mutersbaugh ably summarize, Chayanov's "basic claim was that family production precluded analysis according to either neoclassical or Marxist canons because both assume a fundamental distinction between capital and labor and between production and reproduction that do not exist within family farms."[26]

Relative to Ricardo, Chayanov notes that the standard economic calculation for any capitalist economic unit would be:

GI (Gross Income) – OM (Outlays on Materials) – W (Wages) = NP (Net Profit)

On the peasant "family labour farm," however, there are no "wages," only hours of labor expended.[27] The family uses its labor power "to cultivate the soil and receives as the result of a year's work a certain amount of goods," something very different from a wage. The neoclassical economists would respond that the family farmer should be seen as both employer and worker. Chayanov replies that this schizophrenic theory is a "fiction."[28] He adds:

> A single glance at the inner structure of the family labor unit is enough to realize that it is impossible without the category of wages to impose on this structure net profit, rent, and interest on capital as real economic categories in the capitalist meaning of the word.[29]

Given the absence of wages, the entire neoclassical analytical scheme crumbles. The peasant mode of production also proves to be insensitive to prices and scarcities arising from the interaction of farms and between them and the outside world.[30] In addition, neoclassical economics fails to account for what Chayanov calls "differential optimums," where the optimal size of enterprises differs in various agrarian regions and sub-branches of farming, and at given stages of technology.[31]

Having refuted Ricardo, Chayanov turned to Marx. Chayanov challenges virtually everything the old Communist had to say about peasants. Marx called them "the class that represents barbarism within civilization." He saw peasant society as unstable. As in all other forms of economic activity under his scheme, peasants exploited each other. Some moved toward the capitalist accumulation of land and related means of production.

Others lost their property, descending into the rural proletariat. Since the end of feudalism, Marx said, surviving peasantries merely betrayed capitalist underdevelopment. As a class, family farmers were doomed. The future lay either with large-scale agribusiness or large-scale socialist agriculture.[32]

Chayanov responds that the peasant mode of production successfully reproduces itself; that history is *not* necessarily moving toward capitalism or communism; that the peasantry is *not* disappearing: "the organizational shape of the basic cell, the peasant family labor farm, will remain the same, always changing in particular features and adapting to the circumstances surrounding the national economy."[33] On a related point, Chayanov denies that peasants exploit each other. Inequalities in the countryside have another, more natural explanation, rooted in the life cycle of families.[34] Chayanov blasts the socialist command economy in action: "By what means is the individual worker to be driven to labor so that he does not consider as drudgery the input expected of him under the production plan?" He sees the state-run economy generating "a new class stratification," a fresh kleptocracy of rulers who would "deprive the whole regime of its original high ideals."[35] More broadly, Chayanov shows that collective farms would *not* be more efficient than peasant farms and that the "horizontal cooperation" of collectivization would destroy local rural leadership and lead to bureaucratic inertia.[36] As historian Daniel Thorner concludes: "Chayanov's whole approach—his selection of the pure family farm as the typical Russian unit [and] his insistence on the survival power of such family farms . . . was diametrically opposed to [Marx and] Lenin."[37]

On this basis, Chayanov further insists that it is a profound error to use either neoclassical or Marxist analysis in trying to understand peasant farms. While "Manchester liberalism" was based on—and so appropriate to—the scientific investigation of capitalism, it "cannot and should not be extended to other organizational forms of economic life."[38] He notes the one-sided, neoclassical understanding of *homo economicus*. As an equivalent error on the peasant side, "we would assume that every *homo economicus* without exception is an organizer of a family economic unit, that hired labor and employers do not naturally exist, and that the national economy is formed from the interrelations of these family units." Chayanov offers multiple examples of rational peasant behavior inexplicable by conventional economic theory.[39] Even bookkeeping premised on neoclassical concepts could do damage when applied to noncapitalist entities. Chayanov would no doubt have agreed with the American agrarian Andrew Lytle, who quipped: "as soon as a farmer begins to keep books, he'll go broke shore as hell."[40]

Conceptual Rearmament

Chayanov offers what Teodor Shanin calls a "conceptual rearmament" of the microeconomy of the peasant farm.[41] Chayanov's work includes all the paraphernalia associated with modern economics: complex formulae; elaborate graphs with curving, intersecting lines; and the like. However, it can be fairly summarized through four propositions:

1. *Biology, not class conflict or marginal utility, drives the peasant economy.* Chayanov was a biological materialist, a monist in stressing that economic development rests on "demographic differentiation which depends [in turn] on biological family growth."[42] By family, he does not mean some older (or newer?) conception of a group of people eating from one pot. Rather, he means "the purely biological concept of *the married couple*, living together with their [children] and aged representations of the older generations."[43] Shanin underscores the importance given by Chayanov to a farm's sexual division of labor, which "turns marriage into a necessary condition of fully-fledged peasantship."[44]

Equally critical to the "natural family economy" is the presence of children, and Chayanov assumes a robust peasant fertility. Indeed, his whole theory rests on what Daniel Thorner calls "the natural history" of a family, as rural couples marry, bear an average of nine children, settle those children on the land, and then retire.[45] Economic historian Mark Harrison summarizes:

> Peasant economy reproduces itself through the family. The family is the progenitor of the family life-cycle and of population growth. It is the owner of property. As such, it expresses the fact that the aim of production is household consumption, not feudal rent or bourgeois profit.[46]

2. *Peasants seek subsistence, rather than accumulation.* Chayanov builds his model "on the concept of the peasant farm as a family labor farm in which the family, as a result of its year's labor, receives a single labor income and weighs its efforts against the material results obtained."[47] This means that the use-value of a product, or family consumption needs, takes precedence over market value. This also means that the peasantry itself determines price and "factor substitution," again underscoring a lack of interest in profit and accumulation. When subsistence needs run beyond a family's farm product, peasants turn "to craft, trades, and other non-agricultural earnings to attain the economic equilibrium not fully met by farm income." Chayanov concludes that this balance between agricultural and craft work forms "a single equilibrium."[48]

3. *Peasant "self-exploitation" is the key labor variable.* Peasants operate in a nonwage environment. The family's labor product, Chayanov says, is a function of the family's size and composition, its productivity, "and—this is especially important—the degree of self-exploitation through which the working members effect a certain quantity of labor units in the course of the year." Crafting another key theorem, Chayanov adds that "the degree

of self-exploitation is determined by a peculiar equilibrium between family demand satisfaction and the drudgery of labor
itself." Put another way, as more mouths need to be fed, as the
number of children and nonworking elderly grows, the labor of
family workers expands toward limits fixed by the drudge factor. Chayanov concludes that "peasant farms are structured to
conform to the optimal degree of self-exploitation of the family
labor force."[49] In this environment, the work motivation of the
peasant is not entrepreneurial. Rather, it operates the same as
under a "piece rate system," where the artisan would be paid
for each unit produced, not by the hour. This allows the peasant "alone to determine the time and intensity of his work."
Chayanov adds: "all other conclusions and constructions follow
in strict logic from this premise."[50]

4. *The Consumer/Worker Ratio drives economic decision-making
within the family.* In direct opposition to the theories of Marx
and Lenin, Chayanov empirically shows that inequality in the
Russian countryside was primarily due to the life cycle of families. A newly married couple without children have a ratio of
Consumers (mouths to feed) ÷ Workers near 1.0. They aim to
accumulate land. As children arrive, this ratio climbs toward
2.0, reaching a maximum level of stress with four to six children. The family in this circumstance engages in more "self-
exploitation" and finds ways (in fluid land systems) to acquire
more land, or to expand work in crafts. As the children grow
older, they become workers as well. The ratio then falls, and
these middle-aged families acquire still more land, since they
now have the labor to work it. As the ninth baby comes, the
early children are ready to marry and find farms of their own.
Now "wealthy" parents launch them off with gifts of land; and
so begin deconstructing their property. As the last grown child
leaves, they "retire" to live as dependents on their offspring.
Chayanov stresses here how family size is directly related to
land use, and how "the peasant provides himself with a fam-

ily in accordance with his material security." At each stage of a peasant family's life cycle, one finds "a completely distinct labor machine." Economic life on a farm resembles "a pulsating curve." Confirming this thesis, Chayanov's intensive research into Starobel'sk peasant households found a strong correlation between farm size and family size. A related "correlation co-efficient" between agricultural income and family size was a robust 0.64.[51]

Beyond these propositions, Chayanov points to certain intrinsic advantages of the peasant economy. First, peasants enjoy the satisfactions of liberty and responsibility. As the economist explains:

> The peasant and the artisan manage independently; they control their production and other economic activities on their own responsibility. They have at their disposal the full product of their labor output and they are driven to achieve this labor output by family demands.[52]

Second, "the very nature of an agricultural enterprise imposes limits on its enlargement," making it easier for the peasant to survive capitalist pressure than it was for the artisan facing the new factories.[53] Third, the peasant enjoys advantages in the deployment, surveillance, and monitoring of labor; put another way, it is easier to keep track of family members than hired hands. Fourth, the peasant family can cover its lack of capital by enhanced labor intensity, allowing peasants to out-compete the well-capitalized farm enterprise resting on wage labor. This surplus of labor also enables peasants under certain conditions to buy out heavily capitalized neighbors.[54] Fifth, the peasant farmer enjoys an advantage in ecological sustainability. Micromanagement—"a union of local farmer knowledge and land-productive capability"—can give family farmers an edge over agribusiness.[55] Finally, the family labor unit is better equipped to survive economic crisis. Following Chayanov, Thorner ex-

plains: "In conditions where capitalist farms would go bank-
rupt, peasant farms could work longer hours, sell at lower prices, obtain no net surplus, and yet manage to carry on with their
farming, year after year."[56]

New and Higher Forms

Chayanov is acutely aware that future economic development
required change in the countryside. To begin with, he is an ar-
dent champion of the "extension" concept, where agronomists
and horticulturalists bring new agricultural techniques to the
peasantry and teach and assist farmers in management matters.
The "District Social Agronomist" would be the catalyst for improved farming practice.[57]

More critically, Chayanov holds that the peasant economic
system could survive in the new century only by building up
cooperatives: another tacit admission of capitalism's special energy. Through "vertical cooperation" offering product processing, exchange, tools, storage, and credit, the peasant could enjoy the benefits of large-scale organization without sacrificing
family-scale production. As Chayanov puts it: "We must hope
that the [family] labor farm, strengthened by cooperative bodies, will be able to defend its position against large-scale, capitalist type farms as it did in former times."[58] Although "small
is beautiful" is a theme of *Peasant Utopia*, Chayanov actually
looks toward the formation of powerful combines. While co-
ops would commonly begin around the procurement of tools,
"cooperatives very soon turn to the organization of the co-operative marketing of agricultural products which they develop
in the form of *gigantic alliances combining hundreds of thousands of
small-scale producers.*"[59] He foresaw here entities such as the original Land O'Lakes cooperative in Minnesota or the Mondragon
combine in Spain, multibillion-dollar enterprises controlled by
the producers themselves.

Indeed, Chayanov even shows how extending the cooperative principle to marketing and technical reprocessing brings about

> a concentration and organization of agricultural production in *new and higher forms*, obliging the small-scale producer *to alter the organization plan of his household* in conformity with the policy of cooperative marketing . . . , *to improve his technology*, and to adopt more perfect methods of land cultivation and cattle-rearing, *which ensure uniform standards for the product.*

This fundamental change within the household brings in turn "a quantitative transformation" of rural life, from "a system of peasant households" into "a system based on a public cooperative rural economy." This kind of "socialization of capital" does leave "the implementation of certain processes to the private households of its members." However, they perform their work "more or less as a technical assignment."[60] These households would form a distinctly modern, tightly integrated peasantry, in some respects very different from the model put forward in *Peasant Utopia*.

It was this vision of a peaceful economic revolution, guided by peasant-controlled cooperatives, that an increasingly desperate Chayanov put forward in the late 1920s as the alternative to a mass collectivization of farms. He even turned for support to the spirit of Lenin, who once remarked that "a system of civilized cooperators" could be part of socialism.[61]

Stalin's Revenge

By the late 1920s Chayanov had made a powerful enemy of Joseph Stalin. As the latter consolidated power as general secretary of the Communist Party, he also launched his violent "horizontal" consolidation of the Russian peasantry. In a speech delivered on December 27, 1929, Stalin attacked Chayanov by name for refusing to accept the theory of ground rent devised by Marx and Lenin.[62] A few months later, Chayanov, Kondratiev, and other colleagues were arrested. Stalin's prosecutors charged that they were "wreckers" and members of a secret counter-revolutionary group, the Labour Peasant Party. Condemned to the gulag, Chayanov died near Alma Alta in 1939, martyr for a Third Way economics.

He left a significant intellectual legacy. Translation of his basic work into English in 1966 was a major stimulus to the revival of academic interest in the peasantry during the late 1960s and 1970s, evidenced most notably in the launching of the *Journal of Peasant Studies.* James Scott's influential 1976 volume *The Moral Economy of the Peasant* drew heavily on Chayanov's framework.[63] Recent national and international activism to protect family farming, such as the protests of the controversial international peasant organization Via Campesina, claims Chayanov as an inspiration. Via Campesina seeks "just prices" for farm goods, declares "local food" to be a human right, and—in opposing the World Trade Organization—advances the idea of "food sovereignty." It is difficult to judge how Chayanov would react to this language. However, he probably would agree with one sympathetic commentator that "[s]tate and market—the antagonists of old—still threaten peasant livelihood today, along with the new superstate forms of government."[64]

All the same, the premature end of his theoretical work was a deep loss. Chayanov was an innovator, moving not only toward a general theory of peasant economy, but also to a broader theory of the natural family economy. He exposed how both neoclassical and Marxist theory largely ignored family relations and their powerful economic consequences. He placed the natural family at the core of his analysis, and began to see the vast ramifications of so doing. Chayanov's arrest put an end to this quest. A half-century would pass before economists such as Gary Becker returned to the question. The gulag also denied Chayanov the grand opportunity to test his theory of future peasant economic development in his native land, where it would surely have enjoyed popular support.

Another aspect of the tragedy of Chayanov is pithily captured by economic historian Mark Harrison. "Perhaps Chayanov was the Newton of agrarian societies," he writes. "The trouble is that today we believe in relativity."[65] Chayanov's moral economy premised on the natural family finds too little resonance in a civilization largely given over to an amplified moral individualism and an unsettled postfamilial order.

4

Green Rising:

The Promise and Tragedy

of Peasant Rule in Eastern Europe

G. K. Chesterton could hardly contain his glee. Distributism, his economic project built on a "third way" between liberal capitalism and communism and involving a democratic redistribution of property, was finding concrete success in unlikely places. "[T]he great modern movement is Agrarian," he wrote, "inspired by the elemental ethics of the field." Throughout Eastern Europe and the Balkans, "[i]n a sort of awful silence the peasantries have fought one vast and voiceless pitched battle with Bolshevism and its twin brother, which is Big Business, and the peasantries have won." Chesterton compared this "Green Rising" to the Great War and underscored its historical significance:

> It is a huge historical hinge and turning point, like the conversion of Constantine or the French Revolution. . . . [W]hat has happened in Europe since the war has been a vast victory for the peasant, and therefore a vast defeat both for the communists and the capitalists.[1]

Author and ruralist Helen Douglas-Irvine concurred: "It has been an effect of the revolution let loose by the Great War, that the strength of the peasant class has been revealed."[2] Historians Robert Bideleux and Ian Jeffries describe an unprecedented "groundswell of peasant-based movements right across Europe, from Ireland and Scandinavia through Germany to the Slav world."[3]

Indeed, this Green Rising saw agrarian parties and their radical program of land redistribution come to power in Bulgaria, Poland, Romania, Czechoslovakia, and Finland and strongly influence events in the Baltic states and Yugoslavia. To observers in the 1920s, the future of Eastern Europe seemed to lie with the peasant "Green," not the Bolshevik "Red." And yet, this remarkable episode in Third Way politics and economics was largely crushed by the early 1930s, and is now mostly forgotten. What were the sources of the Green Rising? How realistic was its political potential? What was its program? And why did it fail?

Peasant Masses in Ferment

Anthropologist Robert Redfield defines the peasantry as "rural people who control and cultivate their land for subsistence and as part of a traditional way of life and who look to and are influenced by gentry or townspeople whose way of life is like theirs but in a more civilized form."[4] To the interwar English journalist H. Hessell Tiltman, "the true peasant is he to whom the soil is sacred and the plough the symbol of life." In 1920, east of Vienna and Berlin and west of the new Soviet Union were counted 100 million peasants, an "essential community of interest" that bound "peoples of widely varying race, religion, and language." While a few peasants held farms over 120 acres in size, the vast majority were on small farms of twelve to twenty acres, where their focus was on family-centered production and self-sufficiency.[5]

With the collapse of the German, Russian, Austro-Hungarian, and Ottoman monarchies in 1912–18, and the simultaneous eclipse of the landed nobility, this great peasant body formed an absolute or near majority in all of the successor states. "The masses were in ferment and the monarchs in flight," as one commentator wrote.[6] Peasants constituted 82.4 percent of the population in Bulgaria, 80 percent in Romania and Yugoslavia, 75 percent in Poland, 60 percent in Hungary, and 40 percent in Czechoslovakia. The revolutionary turn by these nations to parliamentary rule and universal adult suffrage gave the peasantry an overwhelming electoral advantage.

However, the peasants also inherited difficult political and economic circumstances. Real democracy was altogether new in these places; the fair competition of political parties was untested. By 1920 the Bolshevik Revolution in Russia had largely crushed its internal opposition and was eager to create Marxist regimes in nearby lands. Economically, the collapse of the empires—particularly of Austria-Hungary—replaced common markets with new national boundaries and tariff walls. This change revealed the inefficiencies of the great landed estates. In Romania, for example, a tiny *boyar* class controlled half of the arable land, but had only a tenth of the draught animals and an even smaller proportion of the plows in use. Sharecropping, organized through fairly ruthless middlemen, was the dominant form of production.

More broadly, these new nations inherited economies dominated by an urban mercantilism "in which personal and class and nationalist interests were inextricably mingled." The industries that existed tended to be large (e.g., steel mills), heavily subsidized, protected by tariffs, and inefficient. Capital cities such as Sofia and Bucharest maintained "elaborate and costly" bureaucracies and military establishments, all paid for by taxes largely extracted from the peasantry. As the Romanian peasant leader Ion Mihalache once explained, "serfdom has not disappeared. . . . Free labor—but taxed and coerced trading—that is the modern method of serfdom."[7] Indeed, indirect taxes such as tariffs on industrial and consumer goods and monopolies accounted for most state revenue. In Romania, for example, the government maintained a matchstick monopoly. Matches were heavily taxed; flint and steel banned; and heavy penalties imposed for non-match fires. Similar systems governed salt, another staple that most peasants could not produce themselves. As one observer put it, "every peasant is working six months in each year for the tax gatherer."[8]

Agrarian politics had its roots in romantic views of the organic society. The peasant campaign reaped the harvest of various nineteenth-century movements: romanticism; folklorism; the rehabilitation of vernacular languages; the "new literature" of long-suppressed peasant nations; the Russian *narodniki* celebration of rural life and customs; and various Slavophile inventions.[9] For the peasant, land was a "sacred thing" bound to the history and future of a family. The peasantry formed the "soul" and foundation of all emerging East European nations. As the Romanian theorist Constantin Stere, writing in 1907, put it: "The peasantry, as the undifferentiated base of society, constitutes a separate social category, upon whose back are raised all other social classes, not excepting even the industrial proletariat."[10] The Croatian peasant leader Ante Radic saw the global "social pyramid" resting on "the innumerable peasant masses of Europe, Asia, Africa and America." This position gave the peasantry a special mission. As the Polish Agrarian party explained in one of its platforms: "Because of their numbers, their physical and moral strength which derives from their association with the land and their value to nation and state, the rural population are justified in regarding themselves as the natural masters of Poland."[11]

Sustaining such claims was a vast intellectual renaissance, with particular strength among the young. From the 1870s through the 1930s, successive waves of university youth returned to the villages "to refresh themselves spiritually by contact with the simple peasants of the earth," to become new men "closely bound to soil and nature." Called "village explorers," they put aside older concerns. In interwar Transylvania, for example, minority Hungarian and majority Romanian youth—communities long seething with hostility toward one another—consciously joined together for their rural pilgrimages. In Poland, the League of Peasant Intelligentsia took form.[12]

Attracting them was a new creed, one which threatened the ambitions and programs of both the Right and the Left. Agrarianism's attachment to family-held property was stronger than that of any conservative party. It shared liberalism's full embrace of democracy and opposition to state intervention into the lives of persons and groups. And the movement's social ideals, together with parts of its economic project, were similar to socialism. In each case, however, there was a vital difference, a novelty that underscored a fresh and exciting campaign with universal ambitions. As the Czech agrarian leader Milan Hodza explained in 1925: "We know that Agrarian democracy . . . is the strong bond which will create of the peoples an international unity, a formal, organic and psychological unity against which all attacks, whether directed by the imperialist right or the bolshevist left will be shattered."[13] When peasant political leaders came together in 1923 to form the Green International in Prague, the organization appealed to "the idea of universal Agrarianism," defined as

the desire to renew and preserve humanity on the basis
of the natural law which reigns between man and the
soil. This law is the chief motivating force in all the
efforts of man to develop himself peacefully. . . . Thus
the man living on the soil is and must be the creative
element in the state. He is always a positivist, a creator
of values. . . .[14]

At the height of his power in 1922, the Bulgarian peasant
leader Alexander Stamboliski laid out a vision for his land, to be
achieved after another twenty years of agrarian rule. Bulgaria
would be a "model agricultural state," a land of gardens, with
its villages and towns free of both muddy, crooked streets and
"human bloodsuckers," the middlemen and the usurers. The
villages would have drinkable water, wooded parks, modern
fertilizers, telephones, electric lights, and railway connections.
Effective cooperatives would insure fair prices for the sale of
agricultural products and for the purchase of consumer goods.
There would be efficient local courts, from which lawyers
would be banned. There would be local schools under village
control. Every village would also have a "Home of Agrarian
Democracy," a cultural center featuring lectures, plays, and
films. And women would hold the vote and gain for themselves
a central place in public life.[15]

Curiously, this agrarian vision and the remarkable political
episode it inspired have drawn mostly scorn from journalists
and historians. Setting the pattern was an early volume by Paul
Gentizon, the Balkan correspondent for *Le Temps*. He describes
Stamboliski as "a corrupt, ignorant demagogue" who hated cities and sought to destroy businessmen and intellectuals. Agrarians in general were foes of the modern world, arrogant bar-
barians.[16] More recently, English historian Hugh Seton-Watson
has mocked the myth of the East European peasantry. Instead
of wearing colorful national costumes, most were clothed in

rags. Few had shoes. The peasants' homes were "hovels." The food they ate was bad: rye instead of wheat bread. And "it is still by no means unknown in Rumania, Bulgaria or Jugoslavia for children to be born in the fields."[17] Historian Joseph Rothschild condemns the "particular irrelevance" of the Green International, the "sad spectacle," excessive nationalism, "general inadequacy," and "naïveté" of the peasant politicians, and the overall "apathy, alienation, and rancor" of the European peasantry. He sees the agrarian platform as a degenerate, "brutal externalization of hitherto frustrated peasant resentments," and peasantist institutions such as Bulgaria's Orange Guard as "fascistic."[18] Historian George D. Jackson Jr. largely concurs. He says that the East European peasants used the ballot "to drag society backward," adding that whenever "peasants can vote . . . they bring their ignorance and irresponsibility into the political process, encouraging demagoguery. They tend to be a corrupting influence." Peasant writers and theorists were only a "quasi-intelligentsia" who sought social status by taking on the appearance of education. Jackson concludes that interwar European agrarianism was almost "a reversion to the fertility cults of the past."[19]

Seeking Social Justice

Are these charges fair? Some do contain surface truths. It is true, for example, that agrarian rhetoric frequently took urban life to task. Stamboliski regularly denounced the "parasites" found in the cities. In 1920, he even threatened to bring fire and brimstone down on "the Sodom and Gomorrah" of Sofia. While this threat stood as something of a joke, Prime Minister Stamboliski did build his own small, official residence in a field *outside* Sofia. Concerning corruption, a few of the Bulgarian agrarians in power proved to be crooked; they were, however, promptly punished. Stamboliski himself was surely honest and lived a simple, Spartan existence.[20] As will be explained later, even the charge of fascism is lame.

Instead, the agrarian program of the peasant parties was a highly original and remarkably progressive agenda focused on winning social justice. It was forthright, courageous, and consistent in theory. Its key components included the following:

1. *Agrarianism is a Third Way social economy, neither capitalist nor socialist.* According to Bulgarian theorist George Dimitrov, agrarianism "upholds the idea of private and cooperative ownership and opposes every form of speculative accumulation of wealth, be it private-capitalistic or state-socialistic."[21] The agrarian author Branko Peself argued that "socialists and laissez faire liberals . . . share certain views on the solution of socioeconomic problems. . . . [B]oth regard large-scale production as the highest form of productivity." In contrast, the peasant parties sought—in economist David Mitrany's words—"a cooperative society, equally distinct from the liberal capitalist society as from the collective society of socialism."[22] The Croatian theorist Ante Radic emphasized how agrarianism formed a "middle way" that repudiated both "capitalist exploitation" and "socialist collectivization."[23]

The agrarians in power were particularly antagonistic toward communism. For Karl Marx, of course, the peasantry had represented everything that he abhorred; he saw peasants as stupid, parochial, and inefficient, doomed by the course of history. The future of agriculture, he held, lay with large-scale, industrial farms. Thinking more tactically, Lenin believed that Communists "must help the peasant uprising in every way up to and including the confiscation of land." However, they should oppose subsequent "petty-bourgeois projects" such as cooperatives. As it turned out, it was the peasant-led governments of Bulgaria and Poland that halted the Boshevik advance into Europe in 1920: in Bulgaria by crushing a Communist general strike in January; and in Poland by shattering the invading Red

Army in May. The agrarian political program also "stole much of the communists' reforming thunder."[24] As Stamboliski could correctly boast: "In order to combat Bolshevism, I have, as one shifts ballast, added so heavily to the social reforms. . . . that I can rightly say that I have vanquished the Communists on their own ground, being more audacious than they and deflating their ideas with deeds."[25] Bolshevik efforts to build a rival Red Peasant International, or *Krestintern*, in 1923 floundered badly; its only legacy was the active involvement of a young Vietnamese Marxist, Ho Chi Minh.[26]

2. *Agrarianism builds on human instinct and social evolution.* Agrarians rested their theories of human nature and history on the science of their day. In his 1909 "new charter myth" of agrarianism, titled "Political Parties or Estatist Organizations," Stamboliski adapted the concept of social evolution from Charles Darwin and Lewis Henry Morgan (author of *Ancient Society*). From William James's *Principles of Psychology* he drew the idea that property-holding was a basic human instinct. Indeed, Stamboliski argued that humans had three basic instincts, rooted in nature: self-preservation; reproduction; and acquisition. These find expression in human society through, respectively, the state, the family, and private property. Marxism errs in attacking private property. Capitalism errs by ignoring or undermining the family.[27] As Dimitrov put it, agrarianism "relies on the biological principle for the explanation of the historical, social and economic complexes of life." The emphasis was on "the living force of instinct"; "instead of history elucidating sociology, sociology based on biology will elucidate history." Society was now evolving toward the satisfaction of human instinct. Appealing to this "bio-materialism," Dimitrov concluded, "Agrarianism agrees [with Marxism] that the capitalistic structure is 'pregnant,' but it is with cooperativism, not with communist socialism."[28]

3. *The family is the fundamental social and economic unit.* Examining peasant-folk society, Irwin Sanders and Clayton

Whipple underscored that "all of [its] life is strongly colored by the man-land relationships," a bond which emphasizes "fertility of soil as well as fertility of women." In the peasant community, "the family comes first, the individual second." Custom governs family relations while older kin guide the young in the selection of mates. The peasant family displays a clear division of labor, based on age, sex, and one's status in the family. Importantly, the family also stands as the chief economic unit in peasant society, featuring a self-contained home economy which provides its own food and a substantial share of its clothing, furniture, and so on.[29] As Peselj summarized, "[i]n rural society it is not the individual but the family which constitutes the basic social and economic unit."[30] Not surprisingly, the Romanian reforms of 1918–20, which delivered land ownership to millions of peasants, were accompanied by a dramatic increase in the rural marriage rate.[31]

4. *"Land should belong to those who till it."* This demand from land-hungry peasants fueled a massive redistribution of land between 1918 and 1930; property passed from kings, nobles, landlords, monasteries, and the state to landless families. Over twenty million acres changed hands. Behind this move lay the assumption that peasant agriculture would not be displaced by large-scale farming. Stamboliski cited Edward Bernstein, who had noted the "obstinate" survival of the German peasantry.[32] In part, agrarians also saw this as simple justice. As one Peasant Manifesto declared, "we cannot tolerate the existence of multitudes of landless men, or men with too little land, side by side with the existence of large estates."[33] In addition, they rested this demand on the theory of "labor property," which stood in contrast to the speculative property of capitalism and the communal property of socialism. As Dimitrov put it, the "private right over the fruits of one's labor is deep in human nature—it is a biological characteristic." Offering a guide to property distribution, the Bulgarian theorist Raiko Daskalov

stated that "[n]o one must have more land than he and his family can work. Everyone must have enough land to provide work for his family and to be self supporting."[34] In opting for family-scale, self-sufficient farming, the agrarians asserted that intensive farming, particularly of the sort involving animal care, was more efficient than large-scale operations. Moreover, while industrial agriculture impoverished the soil, the peasant conserved it; as Mitrany explained, "how could a peasant, who expects to raise generations on the same piece of ground, treat his land otherwise than as a living thing?"[35] The "labor property" theory meant that the value of land "should not be determined by its market price" and that it should "not be subject to speculative transfer."[36] The quantity of labor supplied, not external demand, would fix the price of land.

5. *All families should hold property and strive for self-sufficiency.* For the agrarians, property ownership by all was a political imperative if the goal was true liberty. "If the individual does not possess property of his own . . . , he is not free," Dimitrov intoned.[37] Looking beyond the bucolic, a peasant's farm, an artisan's shop and tools, and an intellectual's books were all different forms of "labor property" deserving protection. And while the agrarians treasured property, they denied that there is a right to unlimited property accumulation. In Sofia and other Bulgarian towns, for example, the peasant government—facing a war-induced housing shortage—fixed a maximum size for apartments: one room for a single person; two rooms with a kitchen for families; and one additional room for every two children over age fourteen. An urban housing commissioner could evict apartment dwellers who held more and turn the space over to the homeless.[38] In the long run, the agrarians believed "that everyone should own the home in which he lives," and peasant governments did provide "substantial credits" for the building of new family houses.[39] As they refined their view of industry, the agrarians also advocated that workers in neces-

sarily large enterprises should participate in ownership of the companies.

6. *The agrarian state welcomes rational and moderate industrialization.* Many commentators, a century ago as today, blamed the rural poverty of Eastern Europe on overpopulation. The agrarians replied that decades of economic and social deprivation and political neglect are the real causes. They were fully aware that land reform, by itself, cannot solve all rural woes. They acknowledged the need for a "rational and moderate industrialization," done in a way "for bettering the peasant way of life."[40] According to one Peasant Manifesto, this meant "[i]ndustries, so far as possible, [organized] on a cooperative basis" that were "mainly devoted to the processing of local agricultural and forest products."[41] The agrarians rejected the industrial policies common to the prewar Balkan states. The massive factories upon which these policies were centered "could have no hope of thriving on external markets," they "impoverished" the very people they were meant to help, and they created "a hopeless, vicious cycle, always dependent on the State and all the time corrupting it."[42]

7. *The agrarian state welcomes freer trade.* While the collapse of the Central European empires opened the way to land reform, the new nations were tempted to build their own tariff walls. Intensely aware of this loss of markets, agrarian leaders pushed to lower tariff barriers and spoke wistfully about building a Danubian free-trade zone.[43] As the agrarian economist Virgil Madgearu explained: "If peasantism does not have an inherent tendency against industrial development, it is on the other hand against tariff protectionism; the creation of hot-house industries, trusts, and cartels." True economic progress "cannot admit . . . a prohibitive tariff system which artificially maintains certain industries" that could never compete on their own.[44] In August 1929, Romania's peasant-led government put these principles into action, enacting a new, more

elastic tariff policy designed to reduce overall rates. It lowered the cost of imported agricultural equipment, reduced levies on manufactured items of mass consumption, cut tariff protection for some industries, and opened the door to foreign investment capital.[45]

8. *The agrarian economy is fulfilled through the cooperative.* The theorist Constantin Stere described the agrarian economic order in this way:

> A free peasantry master of its land, the development of crafts and small industries, with the aid of *an intense cooperative movement* in the villages and towns, state monopoly of large industry (with the exception of special cases which are able to develop on their own without prejudice to the economy): this is the formula for our economic and social progress.[46]

A Peasant Manifesto asserted that the "peasants themselves should control marketing, credit, and the supply of agricultural equipment by their own institutions, democratically organized."[47] The economist Madgearu praised the peasant cooperative, "which guarantees a maximum return and an organization of sales which, by doing away with intermediaries, gives the villager the whole value of his produce."[48] In 1919, Bulgaria's agrarian government created the Grain Consortium, a cooperative designed to raise and stabilize prices. It also chartered cooperative banks, resembling credit unions, to provide low-interest loans to farmers. And it established fishing cooperatives, which controlled the sale of fishing rights and supplied credit for new equipment.[49]

9. *Social justice requires tax reform.* This same government introduced a progressive income tax for the first time in Bulgaria's history. In prior decades, almost the whole tax burden fell on rural small holdings and on farming equipment such as ox-carts and tools. The new law placed a tax on personal income that

rose to a maximum of 35 percent. Corporations, banks, and insurance companies faced a tax on profits of up to 25 percent.[50] As Dimitrov explained, "[i]n this manner, the economically weak strata of society was relieved from excessive taxation and the burden fell on the well-to-do classes."[51]

10. *Agrarianism requires a parity in prices.* Successive falls in agricultural prices create what contemporary analysts called the "price scissors," where the cost of industrial goods rise while the return on farm-raised goods declines. Abandoning market pricing here, agrarian advocates argued that "the peasantry should be assured of a market for their produce at stable prices. This will require regulation both on a national and on an international scale."[52] Or as Peselj put it, a "fair price system" requires "a just return on the peasants' labor and capital . . . and a proper ratio between the prices of Agrarian commodities and industrial goods."[53]

11. *Agrarianism embraces republicanism and democracy.* Rejecting old talk about "God, King, and Soil," the peasants had no use for monarchs and dynasties. It was kings who dragged nations into wars, where the children of the peasantry would die. Praising the anti-royal aspects of the French Revolution, Stamboliski believed that all people of good will had now been drawn into the struggle to replace monarchic absolutism with a system "that would guarantee civil and political rights." In 1918, he declared Bulgaria a republic, but as a political necessity he reluctantly agreed to accept "Tsar" Boris III as a figurehead monarch.[54] The agrarians also believed in representative government based on a universal adult franchise. As Peselj wrote, the Peasant Program sought "a parliamentary regime with proportional representation and competition for political leadership."[55] In Dimitrov's words, "Agrarianism favors a republic that coordinates freedom with social justice."[56] The agrarians also strongly favored such direct democratic devices as the referendum, the initiative, and the recall.

12. *Agrarians see "estatism" as the wave of the future.* Peasant theorists cast existing political parties—conservative, liberal, and socialist—as products of past exploitation and class competition. These parties were incapable of leading nations into the next stage of history. Dimitrov saw "a long biologico-evolutive [sic] process in which social cooperation" played the leading part. Humanity aims toward "a normal social co-operativism." The political parties must yield to "progressive cooperative aggregations" that could create an "equalized republic consecrating freedom, social stability and cultural progress."[57] These new "estatist" entities combined political action with educational, social, economic, and cultural functions. As reshaped by Stamboliski, the Bulgarian Agrarian National Union was exemplary. In addition to fielding candidates for election, it offered classes to peasants, organized credit and marketing cooperatives, and provided life insurance to its members. Wage laborers would build similar estatist bodies through their unions; artisans through their guilds. They would eventually set up an "economic parliament" that would channel national resources into a consistent program of economic development.[58]

13. *Agrarians seek decentralized, localist government.* For millennia, peasant societies looked "with resentment upon the imposition of outside officials."[59] Peselj saw this as a positive, arguing for "the greatest possible local self-government, under which local, social, economic, and cultural problems can best be served."[60] Bulgaria's agrarian regime fostered local control by reducing the number and pay of national bureaucrats in Sofia. It placed schools under village control and allowed the local citizenry to vote on retaining a teacher after a four-year trial. To limit the power of the national courts, it created rural district courts to deal with land and inheritance disputes. The judges would be elected locally. Lawyers were barred from these courts; peasants represented themselves.[61]

14. *Education is vital to the peasantry's future.* Rather than wallowing in their ignorant barbarism, as has often been charged, the agrarians strove to build new networks of schools, extending modern instruction to all age groups. As one contemporary observer noted, "Bulgaria has discovered the vital truth that the key to future prosperity of Agrarian nations is *to be found in education and then more education.*"[62] Historian John Bell comments that "the Agrarians had an almost eighteenth-century faith in the power of education to change society."[63] Leaders recognized that Europe's best-educated peasants—found in Denmark, Sweden, and Switzerland—were also the most prosperous, healthy, and dynamic ones. These were the farmers most open to improved technologies, new seed varieties, better cropping and conservation practices, and fresh approaches to human and animal hygiene.[64]

In Bulgaria, the 1908 agrarian platform called for a vast expansion of the rural school system and a doubling—to six years—of compulsory education. Coming to power in 1919, the agrarians pushed these changes through. The government raised the fund for building rural schools sixfold, to 120 million *leva.* Over four years, it constructed 1,100 new schools. The agrarians also opened five new teacher-training colleges, three of them in rural Bulgaria. They reformed the curriculum to include practical subjects, including agriculture and the applied sciences. They created a new form of secondary schools, *Realka,* which taught farming and handcrafts in rural areas, industrial arts in the cities, and forestry and fishing in the appropriate locales. The agrarian minister of education, Stoian Omarchevski, believed in the educative value of "walks through the countryside" and work on experimental farms. All elementary and secondary students experienced two "labor weeks" each school year and a "labor half day" once a week. The government funded night and Sunday schools for older citizens; adult illiteracy fell below 3 percent. As the Russian commentator V. I. Lebedev remarked, the agrarians "formented among the people the worthy sentiments of idolizing labor . . . and education."[65] At Sofia University, the agrarians also revolutionized the curriculum, adding faculties of medicine, veterinary studies, and agronomy and giving more emphasis to foreign languages, the natural sciences, and accounting.[66]

15. *The agrarians believe in public works and public duty.* Economic progress in rural areas required a massive improvement in infrastructure: "the vital supply of hydro-electric power" and the extension of electricity to all farms; "the improvement of road transport"; and the building of health clinics.[67] Stamboliski's government introduced a startling innovation here, the National Labor Service, which became the agrarians' "proudest and most original achievement." The 1920 law required all young Bulgarians to serve their nation: one year for young men; six months for young women. There would be no exemptions, nor could the wealthy buy their way out. Agrarian theorists saw this as a way to inculcate a sense of duty in youth; to replace the militaristic nationalism of the old draft with training in practical skills; and to break down barriers between town and country. Wealthy urban Bulgarians, "appalled at the prospect of their children performing physical labor," used international pressure to reduce the measure's sweep. Still, in November 1921, the first thirty thousand *trudovaks* were mustered. Wearing uniforms emblazoned with the legend, "By Labor, For Bulgaria," they heard lectures on health and hygiene, farmed state-owned lands, built roads, prepared railroad beds, and constructed rural schools.[68] As Dimitrov summarized, "The cannons and machine-guns were made into plows and scythes, into sickles and shovels, and were applied to building schools, hospitals, reading rooms, roads, and bridges."[69] There was even a "women's rights" component to the project. Male-female relations in Bulgaria were still conditioned by centuries of Ottoman Muslim rule. The inclusion of young women in the

Labor Service was, in the context of the times, a "sharp break" with Bulgarian custom.[70]

16. *Agrarianism seeks peace and disarmament.* Peasant leaders understood that the cannon fodder in any war would be their sons. As one Bessarabian peasant put it, "whoever wins the next war, the peasant will lose it."[71] The result was a commitment to authentic pacifism. When Bulgaria's Tsar Ferdinand made his war speech in 1914, Stamboliski replied:

> We will throw down the gauntlet to adventurists, no matter where they come from, and we will suffer to protect Bulgaria from this terrible danger. And if we fall in this battle we will be content, for we will not live to see the shame and doom of Bulgaria, and we will know that the generation you wish to sacrifice in your adventures will surely pay you back, that it will repay you severely and justly for your policy of insanity.[72]

After the Great War, in both "winning" and "losing" nations, agrarians walked the pacifist path. In Yugoslavia, Stephan Radic put new stress on the pacifist plank of his Croatian Peasant Party platform.[73] In Bulgaria, Stamboliski welcomed the clause of the Treaty of Neuilly which required Bulgarian disarmament. He cheerfully moved resources away from the military into economic development and school construction.

17. *Agrarians love their faith, monitor their clergy.* In a peasant society, religion "proves a bulwark rather than a competitor of the family system."[74] As agrarianism became political, churches—particularly the relatively centralized Roman Catholic Church—posed a delicate problem. In Croatia, the Radic brothers combined reverence for God with a marked anticlericalism, seeking to break the control of rural clergy over the minds of the peasants.[75] In Bulgaria, Stamboliski faced an Orthodox clergy which tended to back "usurers and petty politicians" and a church that maintained large monastic estates. He

called on priests to focus on building an earthly paradise: "It is a duty of these functionaries, who are a burden on the people, to abandon the useless way of life they have led up to now, and to set out on the course that modern life demands."[76] This practical approach to religion carried over to relations with the Jewish population in Eastern Europe. While some early agrarian outbursts—notably Romania's Peasant Revolt of 1907—were colored by anti-Semitism, Agrarian parties in postwar Hungary and Romania "openly stood up against the virulent anti-Semitism" encouraged by other groups.[77]

18. *Agrarians seek transnational union.* Of all the political parties found in interwar Eastern Europe, the Agrarians were the least affected by nationalism. As early as 1900, Stamboliski hoped that emerging estatist organizations would cross national borders. When, five years later, the International Institute of Agriculture took form in Rome, he yearned for it to become the catalyst for a "Green International." In 1923, he cofounded the International Agrarian Bureau, an authentic global "Green" movement. As prime minister, he worked tirelessly to heal differences with his Balkan neighbors and to build a real federation of states. As Dimitrov remarked, Stamboliski "preached of the United States of Europe long before Aristides Briand."[78] All interwar agrarians "gave stalwart support to the League of Nations."[79] Indeed, the dream of a federated, peaceful, and cultured world stands as "one of the grandest objectives of Agrarianism."[80]

The Perils of Power and Responsibility

With this platform, agrarians came to power in a number of East European nations between 1919 and 1939. How did they fare politically?

Arguably the most successful peasant tenure occurred in Czechoslovakia. As late as 1896, 85 percent of the rural population in these Hapsburg territories owned no land. A full third of the arable land belonged to 150 families, mainly Austrian and Hungarian. In the wake of the Dual Monarchy's collapse, Dr. Milan Hozda of Slovakia and Antonin Svehla of Bohemia put together the Republican Party of Smallholders and Agriculturalists. This agrarian party would be part of every Czech coalition government between 1919 and 1938. Indeed, Svehla served three times as prime minister. Land redistribution proved relatively easy here; estates held by the Hapsburgs and "foreign" German and Hungarian nobility were simply seized, usually without compensation. By 1931, 4.5 million acres had been distributed to Czech and Slovak farmers. Dwarf holdings of five acres or less diminished; those of twenty-five to one hundred acres multiplied. Ninety-eight percent of farms were seventy-five acres or less, creating a relatively prosperous and successful middling peasant class and a healthy balance between town and city. Only the betrayal of Czechoslovakia by British and French leaders at Munich brought an end to this story.[81]

A stormier, more fascinating, but equally tragic experiment developed in Bulgaria. Stamboliski, leader of and chief theorist for the Bulgarian Agrarian National Union (BANU), spent much of the Great War in prison. As the demoralized Bulgarian royal regime crumbled in September 1918, he won release. With the military, the monarchy, and the old political parties all discredited, only BANU and the Communist Party could claim popular support. In the August 1919 election, BANU won 31 percent of the vote—to the Communists' 18 percent—and formed a minority government, with Stamboliski as Prime Minister. Seeing an opportunity in the chaos, the Communists—who had their own paramilitary formations—pressed plans for a massive general strike in December. Without a loyal army, Stamboliski appealed to his local BANU councils and raised the Orange Guard, able-bodied peasants armed mainly with clubs. Ten thousand of them gathered in Sofia on Christmas Eve; four days later the Communists launched their strike. The Orange Guard successfully protected state property and kept the trains running. Stamboliski dispatched loyal cadres to the coal mines and arrested the strikers. By mid-January, the Communist plot was crumbling. A new election on March 28 brought BANU within five seats of an absolute parliamentary majority. Stamboliski used loopholes in the election laws to deny seats to thirteen opposition deputies and claimed control.

His new cabinet was young and devoted. Stamboliski's government launched its fourfold program of land confiscation and distribution, national labor service, educational reform, and the promotion of cooperatives. A 1920 law established a maximum holding of seventy-five acres. Estate land above that size, including monastic property not directly worked by monks, would be seized, with compensation paid on a sliding scale. As the BANU government's popularity grew, Stamboliski took steps—including some of questionable legality—to marginalize his political opponents. The spring 1923 election was a "brilliant triumph" for the party, which won 80 percent of the parliamentary seats. In May, over three hundred thousand Agrarians in district assemblies took an oath to defend the BANU government with their lives. One thousand Orange Guard horsemen paraded through Sofia. "Do not think that the government will fall," declared a confident Stamboliski, "but believe that Agrarian rule will continue for twenty-five years. Who can stop us?"[82]

A month later, Stamboliski was dead, his fellow ministers in jail or on the run. Election results had convinced BANU's opponents that only a coup could bring an end to Agrarian control. Former army officers who resented Stamboliski's pacifism formed the Military League; they conspired with the rump Bulgarian army and with the remnants of General Wrangel's "White Russian" force, which had taken refuge in Bulgaria. Leaders of the Orthodox Church, disturbed by the seizure of monastic lands and by the curricular reforms that had reduced the time given to religious instruction, were sympathetic to the plotters. Bureaucrats resented their pay cuts and Stamboliski's ban on holding both a government post and a university position. Police complained of the use of Orange Guards to control street parades. IMRO, a terrorist band seeking to reclaim Macedonia for Bulgaria, was incensed by Stamboliski's friendly overtures to Yugoslavia. Tsar Boris III apparently knew of the plot, but did nothing. Binding all of them together was an admiration for Benito Mussolini, who had recently consolidated control over Italy. Launched on June 11, the coup caught Stamboliski completely by surprise. Captured after several days on the run, he suffered prolonged and brutal torture, and ultimately death. Bulgaria's remarkable experiment in popular and agrarian government was over.[83]

The new nation of Poland, pieced together from large parts of the failed German, Austro-Hungarian, and Russian empires, quickly began to institute land reform under the spur of the Polish Peasant Party, led by Wincenty Witos. In 1918, two-thirds of the agricultural land was held by peasant families, averaging fifteen acres per farm. The remainder was in large, sometimes vast estates. Laws passed by Peasant-led governments in 1919 and 1925 fixed a maximum farm size of 750 acres, provided compensation to Polish owners of confiscated land, and allotted five hundred thousand acres annually to landless Poles. The decree also created agricultural banks to provide peasants with low-interest loans. Between 1920 and 1937, the government redistributed 6.25 million acres to seven hundred thousand families. In 1920, Witos rallied his young nation to repel the invading Russian Red Army. By 1926, reactionary elements in the military and landed gentry, led by Marshall Pilsudsky, staged a *coup d'etat*. The Polish Peasant Party mounted "a stubborn fight" against the new dictatorship. During the 1930 elections, the government arrested Witos and jailed him on false charges. However, a band of agrarian youth freed him from prison and led him into exile in Czechoslovakia. In David Mitrany's judgment, the Peasant Party was done in "by its very moderation."[84]

In Romania, land reform began in 1917 as a desperate effort to raise the morale of the Romanian army and counter the Bolshevik temptation. Memories of the 1907 Peasant Revolt, and its brutal suppression, remained strong.[85] A nervous King Ferdinand now told his troops that "you have earned the right of being masters . . . of that soil upon which you fought. Land will be given you. I, your King, am the first to set the example, and you will also take a large part in public affairs."[86] The subsequent decree of December 1918 granted the peasants five million acres, to be taken from private estates of over 250 acres in size as well as from crown, state, and religious domains. A peasant leader, M. I. Mihalache, became the minister of agriculture and pushed the confiscations through with breathtaking speed. Mihalache declared:

> Our Agrarian legislation is inspired by the ideal that our country is a peasant country . . . that is, a country whose economic life must be based on agriculture, with small property as its typical agent and, at the most, a limited extent of middle-sized property; large property being abolished.

Responding to the Communists, he snorted that "before coming to that distant Socialist heaven, . . . the country must first pass under the sign of the peasant."[87]

In October 1926, the Romanian National party of Transylvania and the Peasant Party of the old kingdom united to form the National Peasant Party. In November 1928, on "a wave of national enthusiasm and optimism," this party won 80 percent of the vote in Romania's first truly free election. It formed a government led by the morally upright Iuliu Maniu. The agrarians set out to stabilize the nation's currency, reduce tariffs, expand the cooperatives, encourage foreign investment, and improve rural roads and schools. Alas, these economic reforms were soon overwhelmed by the emerging Great Depression. Communist-inspired strikes in late 1929 led to the death of twenty miners and inspired "a press campaign of vilification and sensational rumors" directed at the agrarians. In June 1930, the exiled Crown Prince Carol returned to Romania with his mistress—Mme. Lapescu—in tow, intent on creating his own royal fascist dictatorship. When Carol refused in October to reconcile with his wife, Maniu resigned, marking, in the words of one scholar, "the conclusion of Romania's brief experiment with responsible government."[88]

Another tragic political failure occurred in Croatia. There, the brothers Ante and Stephan Radic cofounded the Croatian Peasant Party in 1905 under the legend "Faith in God and the Peasant's Furrow." Stephan Radic was the primary author of the short-lived Croatian Constitution of 1921, which favored the "abolishment of large land ownership in favor of private family and cooperative ownership." It also placed faith in decentralized, local government, called "self governing, economic village administrations." Frightened by the peasants' potential power, the Yugoslav Regent Alexander issued a decree in February 1919 abolishing the remnants of feudalism and expropriating "all large landed estates" for distribution "to those citizens who till the land but do not own any." The landless peasants were granted "only so much land as they can work with their family."[89] However, Serbs dominated the new Kingdom of the Serbs, Croats, and Slovenes, and they banned the Croatian Peasant Party because of its separationist tendencies. While enjoying overwhelming support among the Croats, it never could gain public office. Reactionary elements in Belgrade undermined the land reform decree of 1919, delaying the real transfer of property for a decade or more. In 1926, Yugoslav nationalists assassinated Stephan Radic.[90]

Explaining Failure

Was the attempt to build and preserve a peasant social and economic order in the modern world doomed from the start? Many commentators have thought so. Seton-Watson, after reviewing the misery, irrationality, and poverty that characterized the interwar peasant lands, concludes that by 1939 the situation "of the Eastern European peasantry was worse than it had been in 1914."[91] According to Mark Thompson, "Land reform in Eastern Europe during the inter-war period did not bring prosperity to the peasantry."[92] Rothschild asserts that "peasantism's general inadequacy" was "exposed by The Great Depression."[93]

Compared to what? The "inadequacy" of liberal capitalism, for example, was far more "exposed" by the economic crisis of the 1930s than was that of agrarianism. The alternative push for massive, heavily capitalized, city-centered industries, as favored by "East European dictators, economic nationalists, communist parties, military interests and some influential Western development economists," proved in the end to be a terrible and dirty mistake, one that is still exacting huge economic, social, and environmental costs.[94] In retrospect, Bidileux and Jeffries "heartily concur" with the agrarian argument that industrialization in East European peasant areas ought to have focused on meeting the basic needs of the peasantry.[95]

The crowd of enemies surrounding the agrarians oddly testifies to their real potential. Amidst royalist, fascist, militarist, capitalist, socialist, and Communist foes, "the peasantist movements remained the highest and most authentic expression of [both] popular and intelligentsia aspirations in the interwar period."[96] As Mitrany writes:

> The hue and cry was ever against the Bolshevik wolves, but it was the Peasant shepherds who got murdered, like Stamboliski and Radic, or imprisoned and ostra-

cized, like Witos and Maniu and a host of their followers. In one country after another, the peasant groups were in this way cheated out of their legitimate claim to power.[97]

Why this result? In part because the agrarian parties labored under the burden of a host of innate handicaps. By their very nature, peasants are independent, suspicious, and hard to organize. Gaining political responsibility after the upheavals of the Great War, the agrarians were faced with new national boundaries and old rivalries and hatreds that prevented the needed regional cooperation. Coming to power too early, without deeply experienced cadres, agrarian leaders had to rely far too much on inherited bureaucracies seething with their own resentments and bent on frustrating the peasant parties' every move. Despite being the only viable alternative to fascism or communism, the agrarian governments of Poland, Bulgaria, and Romania won neither sympathy nor support from the Western powers. Fully aware that land reform was not enough, the agrarians lacked the resources (and the time) to encourage the decentralized industries, build the road systems, expand the agricultural extension work, and strengthen the cooperatives that would advance national economies. The agrarian push for lower tariffs and liberalized trade collided with the "imperial preferences" and neo-mercantilism of the Western powers, followed by the worldwide economic collapse of 1929–30.

More fundamentally, the agrarians failed because they were too honorable and decent. Fully committed to democratic rule, they refused to smash their national constitutions in order to hold onto power. (Stamboliski only bent his.) Firmly believing in pacifism, they abhorred and avoided whenever possible the use of violence. Moreover, as Mitrany explains, the peasant political program in its social conception was "as revolutionary as Socialism, and in the face of ruthless obstruction, could have been carried through only by equally ruthless political pressure."[98] Tragically, but also to their credit, this the agrarians refused to do.

After World War II, agrarian refugees from Communist-occupied Eastern Europe regathered in Washington, D.C. In 1947, they formed the International Peasant Union, the new Green International. It functioned for several decades, eventually becoming a curiosity of the Cold War. Even so, the great interwar experiment in agrarian democracy left haunting images of a Distributist order that had, for a shining moment, truly existed. As H. Hessell Tiltman wrote about one nation:

> Bulgaria is a land of peasant proprietors, and that land
> is owned almost exclusively by the people who work it;
> in no other country in Europe does the small farmer,
> employing no labor outside the circle of his family,
> reign so securely.[99]

Perhaps this should be seen as a paradise lost. Or perhaps it remains as an alternative model of human life and development that is still available to other times and places. Even our own.

5

Last March of the
Swedish Socialist Housewives

The nation most often said to embody *The Middle Way* (an alternate iteration of the "Third Way") in modern sociopolitical affairs is Sweden. In his popular 1936 book bearing this subtitle, journalist Marquis Childs describes a nation that had "avoided" the immoderations of both capitalism and socialism, one that had "evolved" between the extremes of both collectivism and individualism. He focuses primarily on the "coöperators," Swedes who wished "to curb the excesses of capitalism—to check the rise of monopolies that imposed high prices." This movement was in an informal alliance with the Swedish Social Democrats, a political party that had by the early 1930s jettisoned some of the more onerous aspects of socialist doctrine, such as the nationalization of industry.[1]

The Childs book highlights the founding of Koopertiva förbundet, or the Coöperative Union, in 1899. In their battle against the corporate trusts, the coöperators sought "lower prices and higher quality" for common commodities, "to be obtained through distribution and, later, production for use instead of profit." They showed "passionate hatred of monopoly control," out-competed capitalist enterprises in fields ranging from grain-milling to galoshes, and generally battled for a fair economic playing field. Childs describes the system in action:

> The Stockholm housewife comes to do her marketing [at KONSUM, the coöperators' store] as she would in any private shop. She has read in her newspaper an advertisement listing the day's prices. . . . If the housewife . . . is a member of the coöperative society, she presents her membership book to the clerk who enters in it the amount of her purchases. . . . On the total amount of purchases for the year . . . [she] receives a dividend of 3 percent.[2]

This chapter examines the ideal human type briefly featured by Childs in the above paragraph: the female coöperator, also known as the Swedish socialist housewife. While engaging the Third Way institution of the cooperatives, the socialist housewife of the early and mid-twentieth century also represented a remarkable defiance of both capitalist incentives and socialist ideology. Concerning the former, unbridled capitalism has always tried to draw all able human beings into the labor market: man, woman, and child alike. At least in the short and middle runs, the housewife represented the inefficient allocation of labor, an amateur generalist in a modern system based on specialization.[3]

Regarding socialist ideology, the dominant view of women's role came from Frederick Engels. Writing in *The Origin of the Family, Private Property and the State*, Engels underscored how "[b]y changing all things into commodities, [capitalism] dissolved all inherited and traditional relations and replaced time hallowed custom . . . by purchase and sale." Even the home became a place dedicated to commodification and exploitation, where the man represented "the bourgeois" and woman "the proletariat." Put another way, the "modern monogamous family is founded on the open or disguised domestic slavery of women" as housewives. Engels concluded "that the emancipation of women is primarily dependent on the re-introduction of the whole female sex into the public industries"[4] and the rejection of the housewife as a bourgeois relic. In the process, "the private household changes to a social industry" and the care of children "becomes a public matter."[5]

However, an older socialist view also existed that looked upon the housewife in a far more favorable way. This orientation surfaced at the 1866 gathering of the First Socialist International in Geneva, where delegates approved a resolution calling for bans on the employment of women, suggesting that women's liberation meant becoming housewives. The measure's sponsors reasoned that working women pressed down overall wage levels and displaced men; in their view, working women were the equivalent of strikebreakers. Later socialists such as Clara Zetkin stressed women's special gifts as wives and mothers. Women deserved the vote so they could bring their maternal instincts to play in public policy. Socialism should reinforce the dignity and value of the mother.[6] At the 1889 Congress creating Sweden's Social Democratic Party, delegates approved resolutions which denied that there was a special "woman's question" and declared that women should stand "in solidarity with their husbands" in "the battle against capitalism." While calling for equality between men and women "as much as possible" in education and work, the clear sense of the inaugural party platform was that working-class women would find liberation in and through their marriages and homes.[7]

Ellen Key and the Supermom

These relatively generous views of the socialist housewife were given a special Swedish twist in the writings of Ellen Karolina Sofia Key. An author on educational matters and an early social feminist, Key understood that any socialist embrace of the homemaker in the early twentieth century required some fancy ideological footwork. To most progressive thinkers, the bourgeois housewife seemed ornamental, superstitious, sentimental, and weak, a figure deserving contempt. Key's response was to summon forth "the new woman": active, rational, serious, courageous, and strong—the supermother.

Key's "new woman" had two theoretical sources. The first was Charles Darwin. Under "the religion of the past" (i.e., Christianity), there had been "the adoration of motherhood as divine mystery," seen most clearly in "the worship of the Madonna." This had now "been given back to the present by the doctrine of evolution, with that universal validity which the thought must possess to give again to culture a centre." Young girls had begun to understand "that their value as members of society depends essentially upon their value for the propagation of mankind," which turned their "erotic longing" into something "pure and beautiful."[8]

Key's second intellectual source for the "new woman" was Friedrich Nietzsche. As she wrote: "The finest young girls of today are penetrated [sic!] by the Nietzschean idea, that marriage is the combined will of two people to create a new being greater than themselves." Praising both "eugenics" and "puericulture"—or the special protection of mother and child—Key lavished praise on the German philosopher, who "has the most profound conception of parenthood and education *as the means whereby humanity will cross over the bridge of men of to-day to the superman.*" This summoning of the "supermother" to raise "superchildren" necessarily involved a strengthening of distinct gender roles. As Key explained in language strangely archaic, even Teutonic:

> She will preserve upon a higher plane the old division of labour which made man the one who felled the game, fought the battles, made conquests, achieved advancement through victories; and which made woman the one who rendered the new domains habitable, who utilized the booty for herself and hers . . . all that of which woman's ancient tasks as guardian of the fire and cultivator of the fields are beautiful symbols.[9]

Key wrapped this reactionary vision in progressive garb. For example, she urged that "society" pay stay-at-home mothers a full, self-supporting wage. Given the "degraded nature" of "present marriage conditions," which allowed "the degenerate, uneducated, [and] decrepit" to propagate, she said that there should "*be no sin*, from the point of view of the race" if "the young, sound, pure-minded, and loving . . . become parents without marriage." Put another way, eugenic goals trumped the need for marriage. She also praised modern sex education as a means for both men and women "to give the race an ever more perfect progeny," adding: "maidens as well as youths must henceforth demand scientific instruction in sexual duties toward themselves and their possible children." Fittingly, the prominent early sexologist Havelock Ellis became Key's close collaborator.[10]

All the same, Key's main goal was to promote motherhood. The "higher development of mankind" required "that woman *in ever more perfect manner shall fulfill what has hitherto been her most exalted task*: the bearing and rearing of the new generation." She denounced "amaternalists," such as Charlotte Perkins Gilman, who saw pregnancy and childrearing as obstacles to liberation, equality, the marketplace, and evolution. Key stressed that a woman's life was lived "most intensively and most extensively, most individually and most socially" and that she was "most free" when "in and with the physical and psychic exercise of the function of maternity." She saw the mother-child bond as "the root of altruism." The physical functions of motherhood were "the fundamental reasons" for the division of labor. Woman's "liberated human personality" found expression in the nurture of a home.[11]

Nietzsche himself, Key reported, had declared that "[t]here will come a time when we shall have no other thought than education," and he placed this charge directly in the hands of mothers. "The mother who is an artist in education" allowed her child "full freedom" to explore the world under her close tutelage. The new mother understood "the enormous significance of the *first years,* when the indispensable 'training' takes place." Didactic education would not elevate the race. Rather, the new mother's "unceasing vigilance and consistency are required in order that the child shall actually bear the results of his actions. What she needs for this is first and foremost, *time, time,* and again *time.*" The new mother would "lead children out into nature," encourage "their love of invention and their impulse to play," tell instructive stories, and "quietly and gradually" initiate her children into the sexual "mystery"[!]. Such supermothers stood as "the most splendid fruit" of the woman's movement, guiding humankind toward a grand evolutionary destiny.[12]

Key believed that human liberation moved on two tracks: "the emancipation movements of labouring men *and* of women." Men displaying manliness held the ascendancy in regard to outward creative powers. Women displaying womanliness held "the ascendancy in regard to inward creative powers." Together, they could build a new order based on a new human type. The sociopolitical goal was this "higher cultivation of the race." Toward such an end, "the *service of mother* must receive the honour and oblation that the state now gives to *military service.*"

This was the central policy goal of Key's maternalist socialism.[13] Only real devotion to democracy and choice kept Key's formulation out of the later National Socialist sphere.

In 1904, the Swedish Social Democratic Women's League introduced a monthly magazine, *Morgonbris* (translated as "Morning Breeze"). Ellen Key's influence on the publication was immediate and profound. As the inaugural issue proclaimed: "There is a close bond between Ellen Key's ideal goals and the movement growing among working women, in the quest for a higher womanhood." While the journal also carried articles discussing women's right to work and the ideal operation of daycare centers, the dominant themes were inspired by Key. Under editor Rut Gustavsson, *Morgonbris* "sought to shape a new ideal woman, who was not the pathetic home slave nor the weary factory worker, but almost a super-woman of the Nietzschean sort."[14]

Illustrations for the journal featured muscular, beautiful women, "wild and powerful," hair tossing in the wind, surrounded by swarms of healthy, happy children. Articles emphasized women's role as home educators, with a particular emphasis on the outdoors and nature. In 1926, *Morgonbris* editorialized that in "a capitalist state" a married woman ought to have the right to employment on terms equal to that of men. However, "in a socialist state this will not be necessary." For the true goal of socialism was to achieve "the protection of women and children," which among other things meant keeping them out of the factories. With this in mind, the Swedish socialist housewives made common policy cause at times with the more bourgeois Swedish National Union of Housewives.[15]

Alva Myrdal's Challenge

The housewives' domination of Swedish policymaking faced a severe challenge during the 1930s. The protagonist was Alva

Reimer Myrdal. Reared in a stridently atheist, socialist, and feminist home, Alva Reimer met her future husband Gunnar Myrdal in 1919. Married five years later, they formed a powerful intellectual partnership. Following study at the University of Stockholm and in England, the pair won Rockefeller Foundation fellowships in 1929 for a year of research in America. Alva Myrdal focused on early childhood education and "the school as a substitute for the family." She burst onto Sweden's public scene in 1932 with plans for construction of a Collective House that would embody her feminist social and educational theories.

Myrdal's historical arguments resembled those of Engels. The old family structure resting on the housewife and the mother-in-the-home was a fading artifact of history, she said. In the preindustrial world, the relationship between men and women had been in harmony. Both husband and wife worked on their small farm or in the artisan's shop. Then came industrialization, which severed the family home from work. This structural shift, Myrdal explained, had left women in empty, deserted places without productive activity. Rather than becoming Neitzschean supermothers, though, housewives tended under modern circumstances to grow indolent, fat, and self-absorbed. The reality of birth control in conjunction with the "gloomy solitude" of the industrial-era home brought a precipitous fall in Sweden's birthrate. Private housekeeping by housewives increasingly stood as irrational, unproductive, and a hindrance to personal and social development.[16]

The alternative was to build Collective Houses, places which recognized that "work, productive work, is a woman's demand, and as such a social fact." Presenting a plan developed in conjunction with young architect Sven Markelius, Myrdal described a high-rise building in a park-like setting. "Family units" would contain closets, a bathroom, a dumbwaiter, cupboard space, and bedrooms for adults and larger children. There would be a central kitchen where all food would be prepared, either for distribution via the dumbwaiter or for consumption in the central dining hall. Also organized on a collective basis would be sunrooms, lounges, game rooms, libraries, gyms, storage facilities, and telephone centers. Of greatest importance would be the collective nursery. The infants' section would provide twenty-four-hour-a-day care for children, from birth through age two. The nursery section would care for children through age five, serving as both preschool and daycare center, for "the little modern family" failed to provide children with sufficient peer interaction.[17] As Myrdal elaborated in subsequent articles and lectures: "the modern miniature family is . . . an abnormal situation for a child." All small children needed four to six hours daily of being with others their age, so they could be raised to become "effective members of society, not overexcited homebodies."[18]

In 1934, Alva Myrdal coauthored with her husband a blockbuster political treatise, *Kris I befolkningsfrågan* (*Crisis in the Population Question*). The book used the plummeting Swedish birthrate to demand a radical shift in public policy. Arguing that the breadwinner-homemaker family model was doomed to irrelevance and sterility, they called for a new family form. All able adults—men and women, husbands and wives—would be employed outside the home and all the costs of childrearing would be socialized. This latter change, the Myrdals reasoned, would eliminate the "living standard penalty" imposed on young couples by children. Moreover, state-provided health care, dental care, education, daycare, breakfasts and lunches, clothing, and summer camps would allow for planned efficiencies and rational design in both production and consumption. As with Ellen Key, the deeper goal was to produce a new human type: this time "cooperative, socialist, androgynous man." As the Myrdals explained:

> In the new family, . . . the wife will stand as a comrade with her husband in productive labor. . . . During working hours, . . . the family will be divided to accommodate the broader division of labor in industrialized society: working adults must be at their jobs; the children must play, eat, sleep, and go to school. Shared housing, shared free time, together with that elusive, subtle personal bond that is, we believe, a constituent element of the family, will remain. However, maintaining a private household, individualistic parental authority, and the sheltered life of the wife will not remain. They must be driven out of the picture to allow the family's adaptation to new social developments.[19]

And if the latter point was still too subtle for the housewives, the Myrdals were more explicit: "Clearly housework still offers possibilities, as both a mother or a servant, for frail, imbecilic, lazy, unambitious, or generally less well endowed persons to get on with life. Also, full-time and especially part-time prostitution is an escape route always open."[20]

The Myrdals won ideological control of the Royal Population Commission of 1935, which produced eighteen major reports over the next three years. Subjects included housing, nutrition, maternal health care, ethics, family taxation, marriage loans, home aid to mothers, contraception, abortion, sterilization, children's clothing, women's right to work, daycare, and rural depopulation. Except for the final report, all of these papers followed what came to be called "the Myrdal line," and all presumed the antiquated nature and irrelevance of the Swedish socialist housewife.[21]

Revenge of the Women of 1941

The housewives soon had their revenge. Working through other politicians, they eventually undermined the Myrdals' influence within the 1935 Population Commission. Obstensible commission chairman Nils Wohlin drafted the *Final Report*, inserting numerous references favorable to the housewives. Gunnar Myrdal, already in America to begin investigation of American race relations for the Carnegie Foundation, fumed (unfairly) that the final draft "smacks of Naziism from a distance."[22]

"The Myrdal line" faltered in other arenas, too. In 1938, the lead organizations of Swedish capital and labor—the Swedish Employers Confederation and the Trade Union Federation (LO)—signed the historic Saltsjöbaden Agreement. Fixing wages for the entire market sector, the pact tacitly accepted the "family wage" compensation principle for male workers.[23] In the early 1940s, as Sweden went on a defensive war footing, "Fru Lojal"—or "Mrs. Loyalty"—became a central propaganda figure for the Social Democratic government. This iconic housewife stood by her man in wartime, dutifully produced her brood of children, and was ready as part of the labor reserve necessary to national defense.[24]

This surge in nationalist pathos also led Sweden's Riksdag (its parliament) to create the Population Commission of 1941. Unlike its predecessor, this body was firmly in the control of the housewives and their male allies. Leaders of the Swedish Social Democratic Women's League, the Swedish Agrarian Women's Union, the National Union of Housewives, and the Frederika-Bremer Federation—all bastions of homemaking—dominated the Subcommittee for Home and Family Questions.[25] These women faced delicate ideological problems. To begin with, Ellen Key's female ideal from the century's early years could no longer be fully mobilized. Appeals to create Nietzschean supermothers simply would not work in an era and region threatened by Nazism. Moreover, pursuit of the Myrdal line during the 1930s had popularized the notion of social engineering toward functionalist ends. Appeals to duty would no longer suffice.

The Women of 1941—as feminist historian Yvonne Hirdman calls them—resolved these tensions by throwing themselves into the arms of "domestic science," or modern "home economics." They defined housewives as "mothers working at home" and set out

> to clarify what manner of organizing the home is rationally justified in our times and to arrange it so that the home can provide the sturdy framework for everyday life and the space for an individually adapted external environment that people need as much now as before.[26]

The Swedish housewife would become the vehicle for rationalized consumption in the home. Using the analytical tools of home economics, government agencies would investigate in detail family behaviors. Moving beyond the household budget, this research project would analyze the advantages of buying new products as against repairing old ones, as well as:

> family members' different needs, home furnishings and appliances, and household chores: the distribution of household tasks among the various family members, the labor time required for various purposes over the various stages of the family's evolution, . . . and finally consumer habits, eating habits, clothing habits of the different family members, habits of hygiene, . . . habits of child care in the broad sense, leisure time habits, etc.[27]

A model 1945 investigation of 200 Swedish working-class families by the Social Welfare Board found that they had an average of 6.5 pans and casseroles, 1.6 kettles for coffee and tea, 2.8 frying pans, 23.6 everyday plates, 36.2 fine plates, 24.9 mugs and cups, 19.3 glasses, 33 sheets, 25 pillowcases, and 76 towels.

Of course, the whole purpose of such intensive detail was to defend the housewife by draping her activities in scientific numbers and professional language. As the Women of 1941 explained in their major report for the Population Commission: "the simple solution is to give housework in modern society a place alongside other normal occupations, analyze the special inconveniences and advantages that housework has, and organize it in the best possible way for those who perform it."[28] Toward this end, the Women of 1941 urged an expansion of the state's Home Research Institute in order to provide home consultants (much like extension agents in agriculture) trained in sewing, food preparation, child care, the washing of clothes, housekeeping, and home furnishing. As justification, they noted that women had "no objective, scientifically researched and tested rules" to make even the simplest decisions, such as "what kind of shoes should be worn during pregnancy" or whether to engage in "cycling, smoking, or the consumption of wine and alcohol."[29] To correct these deficiencies, the Women of 1941 demanded several years of mandatory education in home economics for all Swedish girls. While the Social Democrats formally continued to endorse equal employment rights for men and women, this new strategy actually emphasized the training and socialization of all young Swedish women as future housewives.[30]

A serious contradiction lay at the heart of this strategy. The mobilization of Taylorism and other theories of scientific efficiency behind the housewife actually pointed toward a radically different end: the collectivization of what remained of housework. As Hirdman summarizes:

> Behind the efforts to create the well-organized family, in which the well-organized woman as housewife

was the chief architect, old female dreams concerning the emancipation of women in society resided, not according to the Alva Myrdal recipe, but by turning the values upside-down, and making the home the most important element. The norm, however, was borrowed from the "big" world, with a male factory job as the model.[31]

In the hands of social engineers, the pursuit of "efficiency" and "science" would in the end consume the housewife.

The socialist housewives pressed their momentary political advantage. The Social Democrats' postwar policy manifesto declared that "women's work in the home is of extraordinary importance both for the living standard and for happiness in society." The party pledged to support the housewives' work through improved housing, affordable appliances, and subsidies for child-rich families.[32] The housewives won mandatory education for all Swedish girls in housekeeping and child care. They won tax policies that made the married couple, rather than the individual, the unit of taxation, which strongly favored the breadwinner-homemaker family model. And in 1947, they won another key victory when the Riksdag approved a universal child-allowance program, which provided cash payments to mothers according to their number of children. Alva Myrdal had opposed this approach, since it encouraged full-time motherhood.

Renewed celebration of the housewife filled the popular culture. In a series called "To Be a Woman," the public Swedish Radio Service described women's quest for the good life. The inaugural show emphasized a "woman's power to accept herself as a woman, to accept her longing for a husband and children, to be responsible for a home, to be able to give and receive love from those who are in her care."[33] Under the editorship of Signe Höjer, *Morgonbris* found new life and purpose. In a January 1947 editorial, Höjer summoned the stay-at-home mothers of the working class to action: "We homemakers are a powerful working group. In consumer cooperatives, clubs, study circles and at home in the kitchen we have an influence that can be exercised to the great benefit of society."[34]

The April and May issues of 1947 offer a provocative juxtaposition of photos: on the former's cover, a young Swedish woman in traditional peasant garb, standing on a picturesque hillside, and blowing an ancient folk horn, with these words: "Arise ordinary people! Families! The elderly! Do not let Great Capital threaten the process of political reform!"; and on the latter's cover, a photo of young future housewives marching and singing "Under Freedom's Red Flags." The editorial stresses that Sweden's political choice was not "between an unbridled capitalism and a totalitarian state socialism. For us Democratic Socialism stands out clearly as *the third alternative,* which alone can accord humankind *both freedom and security.*" The journal summons its readers to march in the pending May Day rally under the red flags of socialism.[35] Repeatedly, *Morgonbris* emphasized how the Social Democrats were building "a social, economic, and cultural model-state" and that "mothers and children receive special attention in this ongoing work." Oddly—to today's reader—the same issues feature articles on flower arrangement, new recipes, the latest fashions, pillbox hats, and infant care.[36]

Even Alva Myrdal was swept up in the enthusiasm. In 1956, she coauthored a book with Viola Klein titled *Women's Two Roles: Home and Work.* While still giving considerable attention to the woman as worker, the coauthors acknowledge how studies of family separation during World War II showed "that small children need the permanent, stable devotion of one particular person," and that that person should be the mother. In a dramatic break with the older "Myrdal line," the coauthors actually conclude:

> Obviously, mothers cannot go out to work if they are to live up to these new and exacting standards of motherhood. This has to be accepted as the consequence of the existing knowledge that love and security are essential to the growth of a harmonious personality.[37]

This unusual attention by Alva Myrdal to the needs of small children apparently represented a genuine (if short-lived) conversion on her part, not a mere accommodation to her coauthor.[38] In recommending that a mother stay home full-time from the birth of her first child until her youngest child entered school at age six or seven, Myrdal joined—however tentatively—in "the golden age of the housewife."[39]

"Only a Housewife"

By the early 1960s, there were signs of new trouble in this Third Way paradise. At its root was a tension between the socialist goal of "equal pay for equal work" and the reality of housewives at home. The system would hold together only so long as the vast majority of Swedish women aspired to the housewife role and "equality" took a backseat to the job categories, seniority systems, and restrictions on female labor codified in the Saltsjöbaden agreement and supporting state regulations.

Other forces came into play. On the LO's Women's Council, for example, pressure grew to forego "part-time" work for women with small children, since this tended to subvert the goal of equal pay; full-time employment and daycare were the better answers.[40] Meanwhile, the LO's commitment to "full employment" kept stumbling on the status of women. Over time, both labor leaders and government manpower planners came to see housewives as an underemployed labor pool, complicating broader policy goals.[41] In addition, a new generation of university-educated professional women moved into public life during the late 1950s. Some had been schooled in sex-role theory and had rediscovered the original view of Alva Myrdal that women's liberation came through paid work, not the home. They saw housewives, be they bourgeois or working class, as holding an unsustainable position in their modern society.[42]

This breed of socialist feminism focused its ire, in particular, on public policies that provided benefits to women through their financial dependence on men. In *The Changing Roles of Men and Women* (1962), Alva Myrdal lent her powerful voice to the old/new complaint: "Today, men who want to divert female potential to care for their personal wants in marriage receive considerable tax subsidies from the state, whether or not there are children in the family." She added, though, that new "stands" by young activists "have clearly been taken against all 'wifely privileges,' tax advantages, widows' pensions and other social welfare benefits that accrue to a woman solely by virtue of her status as a wife."[43] The Swedish socialist housewife was again under siege.

The last manifesto in that ideal type's defense appeared in 1964. Titled *Bara en hemmafru* (Only a Housewife), the author was Nancy Eriksson, a long-time Social Democratic member of the Riksdag. Eriksson faced the same ideological challenge that confronted Ellen Key and the Women of 1941. How can the housewife be justified in a modern, specialized, industrial economy? The appeal to scientific efficiency used in the 1940s now seemed as tattered as Key's call for Nietzschean super-mothering. So Eriksson crafted a new answer: the housewife is a vital service provider, particularly of child welfare and neighborhood solidarity. As she wrote in one emotional passage:

> When the oaks blow down on the west coast, the topsoil weakens and the cliffs grow cold. When the housewife is abolished, we shall also discover that with her has disappeared much which constitutes our way

127

of life. When every door in a neighborhood is closed between 8 a.m. and 5 p.m. and the houses lie as dead as nightclubs during the day, then must a new service institution be created. The child with a key around her neck must have an institution to take care of her when the school is closed. . . . Not a door bangs the whole day. A small child, who wants true human contact, must wait for his parents to come home.[44]

Eriksson condemned the young female academics trying to push women out of their homes into the rough-and-tumble capitalist world. She seethed over claims by feminist author Eva Moberg that marriage and homemaking approximated prostitution. Eriksson indicted daycare centers, which spread disease and denied small children the emotional support that they needed. She also argued that housewives were necessary for care of the elderly. These women served as a form of social lubricant, smoothing over the rough edges of modern, industrial life. She called for "economic equality" between the mother in the home and the employed mother, "especially when the children are small"; for universal maternal insurance; for homemaker occupational pensions justified by women's prior care of children; and for a tax system that treated marriage as a living partnership, an economic union.[45]

Astonishingly, as late as 1964 the labor-force participation rate for Swedish women remained steady at 30 percent, lower even than the American figure for that last baby-booming year. Only twenty-five thousand, or a mere 3 percent, of Swedish preschool children were in public daycare centers. As two feminist analysts would later admit, the "increasing attention extended to working women [in Sweden] did not result from an overwhelming constituency demand from women themselves."[46]

The pressure came instead from governmental functionaries and familiar intellectual elites. Representing the former, the

Labor Market Board began an advertising campaign in 1965 to lure mothers at home into employment. Two years later, the board's director general declared that women "must be regarded as every bit as valuable a part of the labor market as men." A change in Swedish home traditions to encourage working mothers was "imperative."[47]

Tax Reform as Liberation

Attention ultimately turned to the income tax, where numerous and steep tax brackets tied to income-splitting for married couples did give a decided advantage to the male breadwinner–female housewife family. The debate began in 1962, sparked by an opinion essay in the liberal daily *Dagens Nyheter*. Within a year, that newspaper—joined by the Social Democratic *Aftonsbladet*—had endorsed the alternative: individual taxation.[48] Eva Moberg argued that the existing tax system condemned educated women to "lifetime imprisonment within the four walls of the home." Mathematician Sonja Lyttkens declared that the Swedish tax code had "a large, discouraging impact on married women's labor supply."[49] In 1965, the People's Party—historically libertarian, individualist, and pro-corporation in orientation—also endorsed tax reform: mandatory individual filing would affirm liberty and equality. And it would also be good for business.[50]

The Social Democratic leadership soon fell in line, agreeing with the party of business that recognition of marriage and the housewife in the tax code must go. A joint report by the LO and the Social Democratic Party, issued in 1968, concluded that "there are . . . strong reasons for making the two breadwinner family the norm in planning long-term changes within the social insurance system."[51] The following year, Alva Myrdal returned with her own report for the Social Democrats, *Toward Equality*. With the housewives squarely in its sight, the document declared that in "the society of the future . . . the point of departure must be that every adult is responsible for his/her own support. Benefits previously inherent in married status should be eliminated." It added that income taxation should be based on individual earnings, without preference for any "form of cohabitation," Myrdal's new and deflating term for marriage.[52]

As the Riksdag considered a bill to abolish joint taxation in 1968–69, the real stakes became clear. The key issue, debate revealed, was whether the family was an independent economic and social unit with its own rights and claims. Doctrinaire socialists said "no," for the family interfered with the desired direct dependence of the individual on the state. Pro-business libertarians and equity feminists also said "no," for they saw family bonds as drags on efficiency and individual liberty. The socialist housewives, joined this time by several social conservative groups, said "yes": the family household based on marriage must be defended as a distinct social and economic entity, for it provided persons with a necessary zone of liberty.[53]

As the bill approached final approval in early 1970, Brita Nordström of Näsbypark organized the Swedish housewives' last stand. Called the "Campaign for the Family," it identified the enemy as "young, well educated women, often unmarried or single mothers with children" and "persons in radical left circles with strong communist or marxist-leninist worldviews." Nordström denounced women who "wanted to be men" and the concept of gender equality. Women had "special gifts": "it is women who bear children into the world. Not men. This is a biological function grounded in biological differences." She condemned the daycare policies of the new Social Democratic Prime Minister Olaf Palme, for whom "equality for children means obligatory day care just as equality for women means being 'liberated' from children." Nordström labelled the proposed reform a "tax on housewives." She sparked a letter-writing campaign: an unprecedented fifty thousand letters poured into the prime minister's office. In late February, several thousand housewives from Näsbypark and Västerås marched on the Riksdag building in protest: "History's first housewife demonstration," commented the conservative *Svenska Dagbladet.*[54]

The Real Revolution

Alas, this turned out to be the last march of the Swedish socialist housewives. The next month, the Riksdag gave final approval to individual taxation. Overnight, the housewife became an expensive luxury. State employment bureaus mobilized to find work for the women. Within eighteen months, over six hundred thousand housewives had been placed in wage employment, a vast change in a nation of only eight million people. Daycare enrollment soared. In his 1972 address to the Social Democrats' Annual Congress, Palme announced that he would abolish the party's Women's League, the housewives' last sphere of influence. Women would now be "real members" of the party, he said, dealing with "common issues" alone. Ominously, he added:

> In this [new] society, it is only natural for both parents to work. In this society it is evident that man and woman should take the same responsibility for the care of the home and the children. In this society . . . the care of these future generations is just as naturally the responsibility of us all.[55]

In the words of historian Christina Florin, "The Epoch of the Housewife was terminated,"[56] replaced by the comprehensive welfare state.

The revolutionary vision of Alva Myrdal had been realized. Her curious genius lay in her Trojan horse tactic of socializing home consumption. By invading the home under the labels of "family policy" and "rational consumption," she smuggled socialist forms into capitalist society until they brought the entire system down from the inside.[57]

The truly radical nature of this change can be seen in the peculiar quality of women's work in the new Swedish order. In the fields of agriculture and forestry, the number of working women actually declined after 1970; in private business and industry, it grew only modestly. However, in the service sector (primarily governmental in Sweden), the number of working women rose from 350,000 in 1970 to 819,000 by 1990. Meanwhile, in the education and health-care sectors (exclusively governmental in Sweden), the number of working women nearly tripled, climbing to over one million by 1990.

Tax reform and "family policy" had been used as levers to achieve something "truly revolutionary": the shriveling of private homes resting on marriage and complementary gender roles, and a massive expansion of the state sector, using female labor to socialize remaining family functions. Pointing to the experience of Alva Myrdal, feminist historian Yvonne Hirdman triumphantly remarks:

> New ideas of gender replaced old-fashioned ideas about the couple. We witness [here] the birth of the androgynous individual (and I speak about the explicit ideal) and the death of the provider and his housewife. We thus witness old ideas popping up, ideas that had been buried for decades—but ideas that very quickly found their advocates . . . : people, men and women, eager to speak the new tongue of gender.[58]

And, as Hilaire Belloc would add, people living in a comfortable, late-twentieth-century version of the familiar Servile State.

6

Karl Polanyi and
the "Economy without Markets"

Among the more enigmatic thinkers of the last century stands economic historian Karl Polanyi, author of *The Great Transformation* (1944). An admirer of the humanism of Adam Smith, he also deplored the economic arguments of Edmund Burke. Polanyi could sing the praises of capitalism, which he said had produced "a prosperity of gigantic proportions . . . for the whole of humankind"[1] and had "released a torrent of material wealth."[2] Yet he also denounced the "economistic prejudice" found in both the market liberalism of Ludwig von Mises and the communism of Karl Marx. Polanyi drew inspiration from Christian social thought and yearned at times for "a Christian-spirited guild life."[3] Yet his wife was long denied entry into the United States due to her reported Communist connections. Polanyi celebrated the economic insights of Aristotle. At the same time, he became mired in a troubled interpretation of pre-modern economies.

Polanyi poses other seeming contradictions. Echoing T. R. Malthus and David Ricardo, Polanyi censured England's Speenhamland system of guaranteed minimum incomes and child allowances (which existed from 1795 to 1834) for defiling "the very image of man" and creating a human "catastrophe" of welfare dependency. Meanwhile, he claimed that the economic liberalism crafted by Malthus and Ricardo was flawed at its core and inevitably generated the regulatory state. Polanyi defended "natural" communities such as the family, the village, and the small farm. He also devised a new form of "socialist accounting." As an economic historian, he turned conventional arguments upside down, asserting that free markets were actually *the product* of centralizing states, while efforts to control such markets had been popular movements born outside of government.

Finally, Polanyi was a self-described socialist who has had a decided influence on modern American conservative thought. For himself, he soundly rejected the "conservative" label of his day. As he wrote in a 1941 letter, the British-edition title of his book in progress would probably be *Liberal Utopia: Origins of the Cataclysm*, adding:

> In America, the title will have to be different, for here *liberal* means *progressive*, or more precisely what *radical* meant in England until not long ago. (By *radical* they mean here an anarchist or a communist; while the English term *liberal* is untranslatable into American unless you say *laissez-faire*, or more often *conservative*!) [Herbert] Hoover, for instance, is called *conservative* because he is a *liberal* (in the English sense), while [Franklin] Roosevelt is called a *liberal*, meaning he is for the New Deal.[4]

If his American title had been "translated" in this way, it would have become *Conservative Utopia: Origins of the Cataclysm*, with pre-1940 American conservatism being the prime object of his intellectual wrath.

A Conservative?

All the same, a number of recent writers of conservative disposition have been drawn to Polanyi's work. For example, historian Lee Congdon of James Madison University praises Polanyi for "rekindling a sense of moral responsibility and . . . combating the economistic prejudice according to which man is driven by his nature to sacrifice every human value on the altar of mammon."[5] In his analysis of the status of the family in the urban-industrial world, *Modern Age* contributing editor Bryce Christensen regularly borrows from *The Great Transformation*.[6] Economist and management guru Peter Drucker, author of *The End of Economic Man* and *The Future of Industrial Man*, became a close friend of his fellow émigré from Vienna, secured a teaching post for Polanyi in the U.S., and encouraged the drafting of his magnum opus. Most notably, sociologist Robert Nisbet's 1953 conservative classic, *The Quest for Community*, can be read as an extended commentary on Polanyi-inspired themes. For example, Nisbet argues in his conclusion that the market economy was not a natural development:

> *Laissez faire* . . . was *brought* into existence. It was brought into existence by *the planned destruction* of old customs, associations, villages, and other securities, by *the force of the State* throwing the weight of its fast-developing administrative system in favor of the new economic elements of the population.[7]

In developing this thesis, Nisbet primarily cites Polanyi. In an earlier passage, Nisbet writes: "There is, indeed, a sense in which the so-called free market never existed at all save in the imaginations of the rationalists. . . . Most of the relative stability of nineteenth century capitalism arose from the fact of the very incompleteness of the capitalist revolution."[8] Large parts of Europe and America remained rural and "strongly suffused by precapitalist relationships," which provided social and cultural stability despite the rise of cities and the spread of factories. Nisbet also maintains that true liberty comes from trade-union-imposed restraints on *laissez faire*: "[I]s it not obvious that the rise of the modern labor union and the cooperative have been powerful forces *in support* of capitalism and economic freedom?"[9] Again, these dramatic divergences from hitherto conventional "conservative" thought derive from Polanyi's *The Great Transformation*.

Who, then, was Karl Polanyi? Briefly, he was a member of that band of economic geniuses born in the late nineteenth century and raised in Vienna, only to be cut adrift by the collapse of the Austro-Hungarian Empire and the rise of fascism. This remarkable group also included Mises, Drucker, and Friedrich Hayek.

Polanyi was a member of an extraordinary family. To a person, he, his mother, and his four siblings worked to defeat the nineteenth-century liberal, free-market ideal, in the hope of creating a new society that would be free but not liberal, prosperous but not dominated by economics, communitarian but not Marxist. As Drucker reports, "the market creed of the Manchester Liberals may be called the hereditary enemy of the House of Polanyi."[10]

Karl's father was born into a Hungarian-Jewish home but converted to Calvinism. After making a fortune in Central European railroads, he married a young Russian countess, Cecelia, who was wanted back in Moscow for anarchist agitation and terrorist acts. As a teenager, she had even planted bombs.

This curious couple had five children, all educated at home

(pointing, as the reader will note, to both the promise and the perils of homeschooling). The eldest son, Otto, made a fortune as a supplier of parts to the new Fiat automobile company. He went on to cofound the Italian socialist journal *Avanti* and to become mentor to its gifted young editor, Benito Mussolini. Brother Adolph Polanyi left Europe for Brazil, where he formed a group of intellectuals, artists, and politicians devoted to the mystique of "the New Brazil," the "society of the future." He preached "Brazil's continental mission." Karl's sister, nicknamed Mousie, inspired and guided the Hungarian folk movement that spawned the music of Bartók and the discipline of "rural sociology" and contributed to the ferment giving rise to the peasant parties of the first "Green International." The young Croatian later known to the world as Marshall Tito was a "rural sociologist" and a follower of Mousie Polanyi. The first Israeli kibbutz was modeled on one of her agrarian tracts. Karl's younger brother, Michael, became Albert Einstein's assistant at age thirty and later a humanist philosopher most at home with the ancient Roman Stoics.[11]

Karl Polanyi began his career as a young parliamentarian, economist, and journalist. Following wartime service as an officer in the Austro-Hungarian army, he became managing editor of a magazine called the *Austrian Economist*. When the journal folded in the 1930s, and with Naziism on the rise, Polanyi moved his family to London. As all of Europe seemed to succumb to either communism or fascism, he pondered the reasons for the collapse of liberal societies. He allied himself to radical Christian groups, such as the Quakers and the Christian Socialists, who sought the taming of industrialism and the renewal of communitarian life. Intellectually, he spent these years engaged in a critical personal dialogue with both Marx and Mises. It was in London where he also befriended Peter Drucker, who secured for him a visiting lectureship at Bennington College in Vermont. While there, he wrote *The Great Transformation*.

Liberal Civilization's Collapse

Polanyi's book is best seen as a revisionist history of the Industrial Revolution and as an explanation for the collapse of nineteenth-century liberal civilization. This world order, Polanyi explained, had rested on four pillars: (1) a "balance of power" system; (2) the gold standard; (3) the "self-regulating market"; and (4), its handmaiden, the "liberal state." The weakest pillar, Polanyi asserts, turned out to be the third. As he declares on the book's first page:

> Our thesis is that the idea of a *self-adjusting market* implied *a stark utopia*. Such an institution *could not exist* for any length of time without annihilating the *human* and *natural* substance of society; it would have physically destroyed man and transformed his surroundings into a wilderness.[12]

The author argues that "previously to our time [i.e., 1800] no economy has ever existed that, even in principle, was controlled by markets. . . . [G]ain or profit made on exchange never before played an important part in human economy." Rather, Polanyi maintains that new historical and anthropological research showed man's economy to be "submerged in his social relationships." The Hungarian insists that the natural human economy rests on three other principles: reciprocity; redistribution; and householding (by which he means "[family] production for use"). Production for gain was "not natural for man." In the natural human economy, markets and money were "mere accessories" to otherwise self-sufficient households.

Creation of the nineteenth-century liberal order, Polanyi says, was an act of ideology and coercion, not of nature. "Capitalism arrived unannounced," he notes. "No one had forecast the development of a machine industry." The radical break in human economic history actually came several decades later when legal changes—such as England's Poor Law of 1834 and the repeal of the Corn Laws in 1842—transformed labor and land into commodities. This was the great error, he argues. Labor was "only another name for human activity which . . . [cannot] be detached from the rest of life." And "land is only another name for nature." The view of land and labor as commodities, Polanyi maintains, was "entirely fictitious"—and dangerous as well. "Robbed of the protective covering of cultural institutions, human beings would perish from the effects of social exposure. . . . Nature would be reduced to its elements, neighborhoods and landscapes defiled, rivers polluted."[13] The stupendous material gains of the self-regulating market would be bought at the price of the substance of society, through the annihilation of all organic human bonds and ecological desecration.

Polanyi insists that human beings would ultimately refuse to live this way, creating a historical dynamic he calls "the double movement." Even in the nineteenth century, as the self-regulating market spread around the globe, "a deep-seated movement sprang into being to resist the pernicious effects of a market-controlled economy." The end of Speenhamland "was the true birthday of the modern working class," which became the protector of society "against the intrinsic dangers of a machine civilization." Labor unions, state regulation of female and child labor, the early welfare state—all represented aspects of what Polanyi's followers call "the always embedded market economy." This idea shares features with sociologist Ferdinand Toennies' concept of *gemeinschaft*: the embedded economy also rests on inherited relationships and status. Importantly, this concept of embeddedness challenges a core assumption of both market liberalism and Marxism, which for different reasons reject the efficacy of such interventions. For Polanyi, political and social actions undertaken to shelter precapitalist institutions such as family and local community from the traumas caused by the market could re-create a livable human balance.[14]

Resonant Themes

Within this broad argument, there are four Polanyi themes that have had special resonance with modern conservative sentiment:

1. *Unease over "homo economicus."* Polanyi rejects Adam Smith's concept of the "bartering savage," humankind's presumed natural "propensity to barter, truck, and exchange one thing for another." Indeed, Polanyi concludes that Smith's "suggestions about the economic psychology of early man were as false as Rousseau's were on the political psychology of the savage."[15] In place of "economic man," Polanyi repairs to a much older argument, embracing Aristotle's contention that "man is a social animal":

> The outstanding discovery of recent historical and anthropological research is that man's economy, as a rule, is submerged in his social relationships. He does not act so as to safeguard his individual interest in the possession of material goods; he acts so as to safeguard his social standing, his social claims, his social assets.[16]

Smith's "economic man" only emerged in the nineteenth century, when legal changes transformed "the natural and human substance of society into commodities." In Polanyi's view, this led to the degradation of both. By the 1840s, he writes, England's industrial towns had become "a cultural wasteland": "Dumped into this bleak slough of misery, the immigrant peasant or even the former yeoman or copyholder was soon transformed into a non-descript animal of the wild."[17] The mistake lay in the one-dimensional premise of "economic man," a view of human nature that ignored the spiritual and social aspects of humankind. Polanyi offers instead a philosophy of *gemeinschaft*, of community, in which the claims of human society and nature rival, and at times take precedence over, the claims of the individual.[18]

2. Doubts about the core assumptions of liberal economic doctrine.
Despite his rejection of Smith's paleo-anthropology, Polanyi
mostly praises *The Wealth of Nations*. He notes that the book had
appeared in 1776, before both the rise of the great factories and
the advent of the Speenhamland system. For Smith, wealth was
"merely an aspect of the life of the community, to the purposes
of which it remained subordinate." Polanyi continues:

> In [Smith's] view nothing indicates the presence of
> an economic sphere in society that might become the
> source of moral law and political obligation. . . . The
> dignity of man is that of a moral being, who is, as such,
> a member of the civic order of family, state, and "the
> great society of mankind."

Political economy remained "a human science; it should deal
with that which was natural to man, not to Nature."[19] In a
Smithian economic world, society, family, and children would
all be safe.

Not so in the economic system of T. R. Malthus and David Ricardo, Polanyi argues. William Townsend, writing in
the 1780s, was the first prominent English author to point to
"the spectre of overpopulation" (Polanyi's phrase), concluding
that "in England, we have more than we can feed." Referring
to a tale about the balance struck between dogs and goats on
a Pacific island, Townsend concluded that since hunger "will
tame . . . the fiercest animals, it will [also] teach decency and
civility, obedience and subjection" to the poor. He adds: "[I]t
is only hunger which can spur and goad them [the poor] on to
labor." With the coming of Speenhamland in 1795, the number
of paupers and illegitimate births soared. By 1818, eight million
Britons—over a third of the population—were on the dole.
Misery, vice, and unemployment were ubiquitous; scarcity,
hunger, and overpopulation appeared to be permanent human
realities.

According to Polanyi, this was the unfortunate context in which Malthus and Ricardo formulated their new liberal economic theory. Iron laws of population and diminishing returns took form: "In both cases the forces in play were the forces of Nature, the animal instinct of sex and the growth of vegetation in a given soil." As Polanyi explains:

> The biological nature of man appeared as the given foundation of a society. . . . Thus it came to pass that economists presently relinquished Adam Smith's humanistic foundation and incorporated those of Townsend. Malthus' population law and the law of diminishing returns as handled by Ricardo made the fertility of man and soil constitutive elements of the new realm.

Under this system, "if man disobeyed the [economic] laws which ruled that society, the fell executioner would strangle the offspring of the improvident. The laws of a competitive society were put under the sanction of the jungle."[20]

While "the very image of man" was being defiled by the "terrible catastrophe" of industrialization bound to Speenhamland, Malthus and Ricardo passed over these scenes with "icy silence." This misunderstanding also created "that dismal feeling of desolation which speaks to us from the works of the classical economists," says Polanyi.[21] Malthus and Ricardo posited a new principle: "Harmony was inherent in economy, it was said, the interests of the individual and the community being ultimately identical—but such harmonious self regulation required that the individual respect economic law even if it happened to destroy him."[22] Polanyi concludes "that neither Ricardo nor Malthus understood the workings of the capitalist system."[23]

Marxism, Polanyi adds, was "an essentially unsuccessful attempt" to overcome their perversion of economics by naturalism, "a failure due to Marx's too close adherence to Ricardo and the traditions of liberal economics."[24] As the system of self-regulating markets spread into law and policy, Polanyi continues, so did core assumptions of scarcity, struggle, stark limits, and the peril to public order posed by too many children.

This same narrow economism alchemized the gold standard into "the faith of the age." On this point, "Ricardo and Marx were as one," and "Mises and Trotsky equally accepted the faith." Polanyi shows how the post–World War I nations of Austria, Hungary, Bulgaria, Romania, and Finland "literally starved themselves to reach the golden shores," only to witness the entire gold-based financial system collapse in 1929–33.[25] Polanyi believes that this narrow conception of economics is set against human life and happiness. He argues that economists—and humankind—can do better.

3. *Qualms over liberal preferences for centralization, rationality, and uniformity.* In Polanyi's view, the liberal legal order, like the self-regulating market, is "unnatural." Both were built by coercion, within a grand utopian scheme of social engineering. Their rise was part of "a revolution as extreme and radical as ever inflamed the minds of sectarians." The nineteenth-century liberal order represented a "fanaticism," "a veritable faith in man's secular salvation through a self-regulating market." No corner of the earth, no small band of humans, could be left untouched, for only "a world scale could ensure the functioning of this stupendous mechanism."[26]

"There was nothing natural about *laissez-faire*; free markets could never have come into being merely by allowing things to take their course." To the contrary, the liberal market system required "an enormous increase in the administrative functions of the state." A central bureaucracy, backed by an efficient "minister of the police," was needed to standardize weights and measures, destroy local restraints on trade, enforce contracts, protect shipping, collect debts, and guarantee an open labor market.

Polanyi notes that the whole social philosophy of economic liberalism actually hinges "on the idea that *laissez-faire* was a natural development," with its foes presumably working to restrict this natural liberty. He counters that "the introduction of free markets, far from doing away with the need for control, regulation, and intervention, enormously increased their range." This leads to Polanyi's paradox: "*Laissez faire* was planned, planning was not." The latter phrase suggests that efforts to stem the social disruptions caused by the unleashed market system were the truly spontaneous human actions.[27] As economist Keith Rankin summarizes the argument: "The tyranny of the self-regulating market can only become the central organizing mechanism if it is intentionally imposed on society by a government . . . and can only survive for any length of time if such a government resists the spontaneous human impulse toward protection."[28]

Not only was laissez-faire a statist ideology. In Polanyi's view, market rationalism could not survive—and therefore opposed—democracy. Popular majorities would never allow a self-regulating market to exist for long. This explains the economic liberal's preference for limited suffrage (e.g., only property-holders), for a weak parliament, and for strong executive and judicial authorities.[29] True political and economic democracy—of the sort envisioned by thinkers as diverse as the Distributist G. K. Chesterton and the social democrat Gunnar Myrdal—would go together.

4. *Fears about families, small property, and agrarian life.* Later in his life, Peter Drucker explained a key difference between Polanyi's work and his own:

> It was my willingness in *The Future of Industrial Man* to settle . . . for an adequate, bearable, but free society that Karl at the time criticized and rejected as a tepid compromise. In such a society—and it may be the best we can possibly hope for—we would maintain freedom by

> *paying a price: the disruption, the divisiveness, and alienation*
> *of the market.*"[30]

Clearly, Polanyi had a different understanding of liberty and a different vision of "the best we can possibly hope for." He understood that a market culture subordinated traditional obligations to commercial success. As he explains in graphic language: "The country folk [have] been dehumanized into slum dwellers; the family [is] on the road to perdition; and large parts of the country [are] rapidly disappearing under the slack and scrap heaps vomited forth from the 'satanic mills.'"[31] Unlike Drucker, Polanyi elevates family, friendship, community bonds, and a healthy landscape to superior positions. Markets should and will exist, he holds, but they should not be left free to damage or subvert at will these primal relationships.[32]

Polanyi searches for his better world by returning to the commonly derided economics of Aristotle. The philosopher draws praise for his "radicalism," with Polanyi adding: "none has ever penetrated deeper into the material organization of man's life."[33] The philosopher made a sharp distinction between householding and moneymaking, and he believed that the self-sufficient farm was the key to human liberty, both economic and political. In fine agrarian style, Polanyi writes:

> Aristotle insists on production for use as against production for gain as the essence of householding proper.
> . . . [A]chieving production for the market need not, he argues, destroy the self-sufficiency of the household as long as the cash crop would also otherwise be raised on the farm for sustenance, as cattle or grain. . . . The sale of the surpluses need not destroy the basis of householding.[34]

The good society, Aristotle and Polanyi agree, is one rooted in households: "The economy—as the root of the word shows, a matter of the domestic household or *oikos*—concerns directly the relationship of persons who make up the natural institution of the household."[35]

Aristotle's economic principles were justice (meaning fairness between persons of different status), self-sufficiency, and "natural trade" (which he defined as exchanges that would move an entity toward self-sufficiency). As Polanyi interprets him, prices are justly set "if they conform to the standing of the participants in the community, thereby strengthening the goodwill on which the community rests." Crafting related language of his own, Polanyi argues for the *embedded* economy, in which bonds of marriage, kinship, and community would mediate basic economic exchanges toward social—as opposed to commercial—ends. Prices of commodities and labor would be adjusted according to the needs of families and neighborhoods. Trade, on both the household and national levels, would aim at self-sufficiency. For both Aristotle and Polanyi, the agrarian household with its family-centered economy stands as the perfect model.

Serving Human Institutions

Moving beyond themes and sympathies, how well have the arguments of *The Great Transformation* stood up over the last six decades? As an economic historian, Polanyi and his graduate students at Columbia University devoted years to explicating the nonmarket characteristics of all pre-1800 societies and to the search for attractive, previously existing models of Third Way economies. They examined what they called "marketless trading" in ancient Babylonia, pre-Columbian America, ancient Dahomey, the Berber highlands, and India.[36] They drew heavily on the work of cultural anthropologists such as Margaret Mead and investigations of premodern cultures in the South Pacific and Africa and among the Native Americans.

Much of this work, when read today, seems unsatisfying, conjectural, at times fantastical. While "market societies" as defined by England between 1835 and 1930 were surely rare before 1800, it does appear that the market pricing of labor and land, trading for gain, and other characteristics of a commercial regime were more common in the past than Polanyi cared to admit. His friend Peter Drucker even reported, accurately it seems, that by the end of his life in 1964 "Karl himself became a deeply disappointed man." Drucker added: "The more he dug into prehistory, into primitive economies and into classical and pre-classical antiquity, the more elusive did the good non-market society become."[37]

Polanyi's *The Great Transformation* has fared much better as an insightful, if incomplete, history of the Industrial Revolution and of the rise and collapse of nineteenth-century liberal civilization. His contention in 1944—"In order to comprehend German fascism, we must revert to Ricardian England"—remains explosive, and illuminating. Polanyi's emphasis on the historical "surprise" represented by the rise of a factory-centered, machine-based industrial order, his explanation of the profound social and theoretical distortions caused by the Speenhamland experiment, his focus on the terrible political price paid by efforts to salvage the gold standard, and his insistence that the development of an economy be judged through a social lens all remain powerful and important contributions to modern thought. So does his potent reminder that the market economy is not a natural or inevitable development; it requires a substantial level of deliberate centralization and government coercion in order to succeed.

The recent, historically novel turn in Eastern Europe from Communist planned economies to market systems has inspired fresh attention to Polanyi's analysis of the nature of a "market society." For example, former World Bank chief economist and Nobel laureate Joseph Stiglitz concludes that "the issues and perspectives Polanyi raises have not lost their salience." Stiglitz notes that "today, there is no respectable intellectual support for the proposition that markets, by themselves, lead to efficient, let alone equitable outcomes." Sounding like Polanyi, Stiglitz writes that "truly free markets for labor or goods have never existed" and that the manner and speed "with which [market] reforms were put into place in Russia eroded social relations, destroyed social capital, and led to the creation and perhaps the dominance of the Russian Mafia," outcomes that Polanyi probably would have predicted. Stiglitz praises Polanyi for recognizing the market as an aspect of the broader economy, and this broader economy as part of a still broader society. Polanyi "saw the market economy not as an end in itself, but as a means to more fundamental ends," including human happiness and social health.[38] A new wave of Polanyi-inspired work has focused on these several themes, and has raised *The Great Transformation* into "the status of a canonical work for economic sociology and international political economy."[39]

His theory of the "double movement" also remains a valuable tool for understanding sociopolitical change. Polanyi shows how (in Peter Drucker's words) "the disruption, the divisiveness, and alienation of the market" are inevitably blunted by counteractions. These include the passage of laws to regulate factory hours, protect workers, control certain prices, and provide safety nets for those buffeted by the creative, wild turmoil of markets. He emphasizes, though, that these efforts at control usefully include nonstate actions, ranging from the formation of trade unions and cooperatives to social and cultural mechanisms. Among the latter we might count the American regime of the "family wage," which between 1900 and 1965—as we saw in chapter 2—sheltered the home from full immersion into the labor market. In promoting the roles of "breadwinner" and "homemaker," this cultural regime largely ensured that only one family member—the father—would enter the market sector: mothers and children were free at home.[40] A very different example of the double movement at work would be the creation of private organizations, such as the Isaac Walton League or the Natural Land Institute, which buy up environmentally exceptional property and then remove it from the marketplace. They, too, participate in building a sustainable order within a market sphere.

It would be misleading to claim Karl Polanyi as a member of the conservative pantheon. All the same, his work has clearly informed and influenced American social conservative thought, particularly his insistence that economics be placed in the service of natural human institutions. As capitalist globalization expands, this lesson grows ever more important.

7

Seeking a Moral Economy:
The Christian Democratic Moment

In August 1992, during his address to the GOP national convention, presidential candidate Pat Buchanan delighted his supporters and appalled progressive Republicans when he stated:

> My friends, this election is about much more than who gets what. It is about who we are. . . . . There is a religious war going on in our country for the soul of America. It is a *cultural war*, as critical to the kind of nation we will one day be as was the Cold War itself.[1]

The term "culture war," so often heard in our political discourse today, popularly dates from this speech. Yet the phrase's true origin reaches back over a century and across the Atlantic. During the 1870s, the nascent German Empire launched a broad assault on religious liberty and family autonomy, a campaign called *kulturkampf* ("culture war").

Perhaps the most important, if unintended, result of this original "culture war" was to encourage an amorphous political movement called Christian Democracy, in Germany and elsewhere in Europe. This experiment, in applying Christian principles to popular modern governance, developed its own history of triumph and tragedy, and it offers lessons for Americans trying today to apply religious principles to democratic politics.

The Catastrophe of 1789

It is said that the Chinese Communist leader Zhou Enlai (1898–1976), when asked what the impact of the 1789 French Revolution had been on human affairs, replied: "It's too soon to tell."

This answer rings true. The revolutionaries of 1789 unleashed passions and ideas that continue their work in our time. Many of them directly target religious and family relations, including the leveling idea of equality, the divorce revolution, secular liberalism, sexual freedom, state-centered education, and communism. The French Revolution also defined our modern political vocabulary: the labels "liberal," "radical," "socialist," and even "conservative" all derive from that time of ferment (for example, it was books by Edmund Burke and Louis de Bonald written in reaction to the French Revolution that first defined modern conservatism.)

So, too, for Christian Democracy, which rose as another response to events in France. As one prominent early Christian Democrat explains, 1789 marked "the birth year of modern life," which he also describes as "the catastrophe of 1789."[2] Indeed, one of the most successful Christian Democratic parties would take the strange name of the Anti-Revolutionary Party in the late 1870s, and would retain it until just two decades ago.

A Politics of Organic Society

Authentic Christian Democracy is not simply another name for "conservatism." Unlike European conservatives, the Christian Democratic goal is not to defend the remnants of the old feudal order, nor existing class structures, nor persons of wealth. Nor is Christian Democracy simply the "rural" or "country" party, defending the interests of small farmers while ignoring the urban, industrial order.

Instead, the movement should be seen as a distinctly Christian response to modernity, one with its own platform. Christian Democrats understand the French Revolution as unleashing an "appalling anti-Christian world power which, if Christ did not break it, would rip this whole world forever out of the hands of its God and away from its own destiny." According to these partisans, the secularism spawned by the French Revolution produced a "system of modern and almost incomprehensibly diabolical paganism." The movement holds that "it would be utterly absurd for a person to take . . . a confession of Christ on [his or her] lips and ignore the consequences that flow directly from it for our national politics."[3]

Christian Democracy formally opposes economic materialism, in both its socialist and liberal capitalist manifestations. In this view, Europe's early-twentieth-century disorders arose from the "exaggerated liberal-capitalistic economic order" of the prior century. As the Christian Democratic writer Maria Meyer-Sevenich explains, "they [Marxism and fascism] are nothing but powerful reactionary movements, grown out of the native soil [*Mutterboden*] of the same liberal-capitalist thinking."[4] Speaking in 1946, Josef Andre offers a Christian Democratic interpretation of the meaning of the Nazi defeat in World War II: "The materialistic view of history is now at an end. What Hegel, Darwin, Haeckel, Nietzsche and Karl Marx strove for, each from his own field of expertise, has been

historically overtaken and destroyed with the National Socialist Zeitgeist."[5] Christian Democracy provides, instead, a spirit-
focused, Christ-centered worldview that would build distinctive political and economic orders.

Christian Democracy stands for organic society. The legacy
of the French Revolution in both politics and economics was a
quest for uniformity, which meant the suppression of diversity,
the denial of "everything fresh and natural." Christian Democrats believe that the spontaneous structures of human life—
villages, towns, neighborhoods, labor associations, and (above
all) families—need protection from the leveling tendencies of
modernity. Only through these organic structures, they maintain, can the human personality thrive. As the French philosopher Etienne Gilson explains:

> From his birth to his death, each man is involved in a
> multiplicity of *natural social structures* outside of which
> he could neither live nor achieve his full development.
> . . . Each of these groups possesses a specific organic
> unity; first of all, there is *the family*, the child's *natural*
> place of growth.[6]

Christian Democrats insist that such groups precede the state.
That is, the law does not create families and towns; it finds
them. Accordingly, Christian Democrats favor tax benefits and
state allowances to support marriage and the birth and rearing of children as a way of recognizing this prior existence of
families.

As analyst Guido Dierickx explains, Christian Democrats
view the family as holding both instrumental and intrinsic value. On the one hand, the family is the vehicle for the regenera-
tion of all society:

> The Christian Democrats view the (core) family as a
> privileged opportunity to implement their social . . .

principles. They want the citizens to adapt their private lives to demanding interpersonal relationships. Family life, especially the traditional family life of a married couple with several children, is a first embodiment of such relationships in other sectors of society.[7]

On the other hand, Christian Democrats also use public policy to refunctionalize, and so strengthen, families. When they

would like to entrust more health care and other social service duties to the family, they do so not just to alleviate the burden of the state bureaucracy or of the Ministry of Finance, or to improve the quality of the service rendered to the aged, the young and the sick (though this too is a major consideration), but first and foremost because they hope to strengthen the family. [They believe that] the contemporary family is weakened by the loss of social functionality.[8]

Similarly, Christian Democrats seek to funnel additional modern governmental services through other "organic" structures, notably "nonprofit" and religious agencies. For example, in Germany and the Netherlands, where Christian Democratic influence has been decisive, state sectors now allocate nearly 70 percent of the gross domestic product. However, only 10 percent of this is controlled by the central government. Nonprofit agencies—particularly those with religious ties—provide the largest share of program implementation.[9]

The Catholic Way

In its purest form, Christian Democracy aims at Christian political unity. The Enlightenment of the eighteenth century, which spawned the ideology of the French Revolution, had itself emerged largely in revulsion over the religious wars of the prior century. In that intolerant, bloody era, Catholics and Protestants battled each other. Millions died in this Christian civil war. The modern Christian Democracy movement consciously works to transcend theological differences between Catholic and Protestant by focusing on their common enemy—the "appalling anti-Christian world power"—and by building a common social-political program. Yet there have been distinctive Roman Catholic and Protestant paths to this end.

The Catholic effort had to overcome the view that the Church of Rome, from the fall of Napoleon in 1815 through the revolutions of 1848, was reactionary, favoring the oppression of the people, opposing their democratic aspirations, and ignoring the new problems posed by industrial society.[10] Rumblings of Christian Democracy were heard as early as 1791 among Catholic or, more accurately, formerly Catholic clerics who sought to reconcile the Jacobin spirit of the Revolution with the Gospels. Citing "the luminous principles of Christian Democracy," they portrayed Jesus as a champion of the poor and oppressed, an advocate for rule by the common people. A later trio of more orthodox French Catholic writers—Joseph de Maistre, Bonald, and F. R. de Lamennais—gave careful attention to the new democratic spirit. While Maistre called the Revolution "satanic in essence," he also saw its effects as divine punishment for a faithless nation, and as the ironic wellspring of a new religious epoch.[11]

The revolutionary year 1848 saw creation of "The Catholic Federation of Germany." Designed to protect Catholic rights in any future German union, this "Catholic club" became the "Fraction of the Center" in 1858, and eventually the Center Party. While open in theory to non-Catholics, the Center Party focused first and foremost on defending Catholic authority, rights, and church schools.

The young bishop of Mainz, Wilhelm Emmanuel, Baron von Ketteler, began to shape a more interesting, and ecumenical, social Catholicism. During the Catholic Congress of 1848, he offered a toast to "the plain people" of Germany and declared that "as religion has need of freedom, so does freedom have need of religion": in that time and place, these were unexpected, radical statements. During the 1860s, Bishop Ketteler turned to the "social question." He denounced the development of what he called "capitalist absolutism," called for the creation of Christian labor associations to protect workers, and urged political reforms that would increase wages, shorten the working day, and prohibit the labor of children and mothers in factories.[12]

In 1871, following the German victory in the Franco-Prussian War, the German Empire took form. Chancellor Otto von Bismarck immediately launched his *Kulturkampf.* At one level, this "culture war" aimed at reducing the influence of the Catholic Church in a predominantly Protestant empire. The Jesuit religious order, for example, was banned. At another level, however, all Christians faced new restrictions. An 1871 law banned clergymen from discussing political issues from the pulpit. Other laws gave the German state more control over the education of clergy, created a special secular court for legal cases involving clerics, and required state notification of all clerical employment. In 1875, the empire required that all marriages be civil—not church—ceremonies. In response, Catholic political action through the Center Party accelerated. This "culture war" lasted until 1878, when Bismarck decided that the greater internal threat to the German Empire came from the socialists.

The "social Catholicism" of Bishop Ketteler and the foray into electoral politics represented by Germany's Center Party came together in Pope Leo XIII's 1891 encyclical *Rerum Novarum* (The New Age). This remarkable document testified to Roman Catholicism's willingness to meet the promise and problems of industrialization with an affirmative Christian al-

157

ternative both to the laissez-faire of classical liberalism and to socialism. Arguing that "the present age handed over the workers, each alone and defenseless, to the inhumanity of employers and the unbridled greed of competitors," Leo rejected the wage theory of liberalism that considered that wage just which resulted from a free contract between employer and worker. Leo repudiated socialism with even greater fervor, terming it "highly unjust" because it injured workers, violated the rights of lawful owners, perverted the functions of the state, and threw governments "into utter confusion."

Leo turned to "the natual and primeval right of marriage" and to the family—"the society of the household"—as the proper foundations for social and economic theory. The right of ownership, for example, while bestowed on individuals by nature, was necessarily "assigned to man in his capacity as head of a family." Similarly, Leo declared it "a most sacred law of nature that the father of a family see that his offspring are provided with all the necessities of life." In the natural order, he continued, it was not right "to demand of a woman or a child what a strong adult man is capable of doing or would be willing to do." Women, he affirmed, were "intended by nature for the work of the home . . . the education of children and the well-being of the family." Consequently, Leo concluded, the principle underlying all employer-worker contracts must be that the wage be at least "sufficiently large to enable [the worker] to provide comfortably for himself, his wife, and his children. . . . "[13] This was the goal of the "family wage."

Christian Democracy from the Catholic side is best understood as this reading of *Rerum Novarum* put into action. Indeed, in 1901, Leo issued another encyclical, *Graves de Communi Re*, which openly embraced the "Christian Democracy" label. Contrasting this movement with democratic socialism, Leo stated:

Christian Democracy, by the fact that it is Christian, is built, and necessarily so, on the basic principles of divine faith, and it must provide better conditions for the masses, with the ulterior object of promoting the perfection of souls made for things eternal. Hence, for Christian Democracy, justice is sacred; it must maintain that the right of acquiring and possessing property cannot be impugned, and it must safeguard the various distinctions and degrees which are indispensable in every well-ordered commonwealth.[14]

In 1906, Germany's Center Party launched a great debate on its future. Julius Bachem's article, "We Must Get Out of the Tower" ("Wir mussen aus dem Turm heraus"), argued that the party should cease being strictly "Catholic" and increase its Protestant membership, since this was the only way to keep from being a perpetual minority. Action toward this end, however, was deferred.

A Protestant Path

The Protestant strain of Christian Democracy is strongly associated with the Dutch pastor, editor, and politician Abraham Kuyper. The Netherlands, it is important to remember here, was—almost uniquely—a nation born out of religious sentiment. For eighty years (1566–1648), the Dutch Calvinists had fought the Catholic Hapsburgs for religious—and ultimately political—freedom. The Kingdom of the Netherlands was, most assuredly, a nation with the soul of a church (and a Protestant one at that), with a sizeable Catholic minority.

The armies of the French Revolution, however, swept over the Netherlands, unleashing the "anti-Christian world power." The necessary task became the rebuilding of a Christian nation. In 1879, Kuyper transformed a confessional Calvinist political movement into the Anti-Revolutionary Party. He saw the French Revolution as marking

> the emergence of a spirit that stole into the histori-
> cal life of nations and fundamentally set their hearts
> against Christ as the God-anointed King. . . . In place
> of the worship of the most high God came, courtesy of
> Humanism, the worship of Man. Human destiny was
> shifted from *heaven* to *earth*. The Scriptures were un-
> raveled and the Word of God shamefully repudiated in
> order to play hostage to the majesty of *Reason*.[15]

Kuyper also raised his banner against the intrusion of the industrial principle into local, organic communities. Although writing in 1869, he could have had Wal-Mart in mind when he said: "The power of capital, in ever more enormous accumulations, drains away the life blood from our retail trade. A single gigantic wholesaler swallows up the patronage that formerly enabled any number of stores to flourish."[16] What he called "the iron steam engine" even endangered the family:

> No longer should each baby drink warm milk from
> the breast of its own mother; we should have some
> tepid mixture prepared for all babies collectively. No
> longer should each child have a place to play at home
> by its mother; all should go to a common nursery
> school.[17]

Nevertheless, Kuyper emphasized that there was no going backwards. Those who believed in Christ must embrace democracy and infuse it with the Christian spirit. They must "position themselves courageously in the breach of this nation" and "prepare for a Christian-democratic development of our national government."[18]

Kuyper urged this movement to proceed in cooperation with Holland's Roman Catholic minority, politically organized as the Catholic Party. As he told fellow members of the Anti-Revolutionary Party,

> whereas all the parties of the Revolution ignore, if not ridicule, the Second Coming of our Lord, our Roman Catholic countrymen confess with us: "Whence he will come again to judge the living and the dead." . . . They, like we, acknowledge that all authority and power on earth flows from God and is rooted in the reality of creation. . . . They say as do you that this God has sent his only Son into the world and as a reward for his cross has placed on his head the Mediator's crown. And they testify with you that this divinely anointed King now sits at the right hand of God, [and] controls the destiny of peoples and States.

Although advocating cooperation, Kuyper opposed a merger of the two Christian parties, saying that such a move would be "a betrayal of our history and our principles."[19]

Fascist Interlude and Renewal

These cautious steps toward practical cooperation were as far as Christian Democracy went prior to the mid-twentieth century. In the Netherlands, the Anti-Revolutionary Party dominated national politics from 1897 until the Nazi conquest in 1940. In Germany, the Center Party participated in a number of coalition governments and—following World War I—helped to craft the Weimar Republic. However, the party was unable to weather the economic upheavals of the early 1930s; nor could it prevent Adolph Hitler and his National Socialist Party from rising to power. Following a tumultuous three years, Hitler abolished the Center Party in July 1933. Similarly, a Christian Democratic movement in Italy, called the Popular Party and organized in 1919 by the priest Don Luigi Stutzo, was declared illegal in 1925 by the Fascist regime of Benito Mussolini.

In the crucible of World War II, Christian Democracy found renewal and a new language. The example of France is instructive.

Emmanuel Mounier was a key figure. Writing in *Esprit,* a Catholic journal of ideas, Mounier worked out a "Christianized" version of individualism called "personalism." This approach saw every human person as unique, a "free agent" with "inherent" moral qualities and with rights rooted in natural law. It emphasized the importance of developing all dimensions of the human personality, "social as well as individual and spiritual as well as material." Mounier believed that the full flowering of the individual came only through his participation in social bodies such as the family, local community, and labor association. And he called for the creation of a revolutionary Christian party, one "hard," one worthy of Christ, one "radical" in its social-economic vision.[20]

In 1943, a young Catholic philosophy student and disciple of Mounier, Gilbert Dru, drew up a manifesto for postwar Christian Democratic work. He emphasized the transforming quality of true Christian action: the whole person must become engaged, not just as a cog in a party machine, but as a militant working to build a new France on radical Christian principles. A year later, Dru paid for this manifesto with his life when he was shot by the German Gestapo in Lyons.[21]

The further elaboration of Christian Democratic doctrine came primarily from two journalist-philosophers, Etienne Gilson and Etienne Borne, both writing for the journal *Aube.* They rejected the atomistic individualism of the nineteenth-century "bourgeoisie," which, they said, had exhibited a "narrow," self-centered outlook and had shown "an indifference toward basic institutions such as the family." These writers also scorned the socialists and Communists for their "materialism" and their hostility toward revealed religion. Indeed, bourgeois liberalism and communism could be seen as "two facets of a single error." The task now facing Western civilization was to find a third way between bourgeois liberalism and collectivism.[22]

The new Christian Democratic movement would be openly Christian, but it would be neither clerical nor strictly Catholic. Following the anti-religious darkness of the Nazi conquest of Europe, this movement would instead forcefully seek to unite Catholic and Protestant believers and sympathetic others—Jews and agnostics—in a defense of Christendom as a civilization with religiously infused values.[23]

Christian Democracy sought to deliver both freedom and justice. As Etienne Borne explained:

> Freedom without justice is artificial, deceptive and hypocritical; it can be used to justify the mechanism of the free market and the servitude of the proletariat; such freedom is, in fact, the antithesis of freedom. Likewise, justice without freedom leads to tyranny and to the totalitarianism of Soviet communism or Fascist corporatism.[24]

To accomplish these tasks—to reconcile individualism with community and to deliver both justice and liberty—the French Christian Democrats gave priority to the defense of natural social groups. As Borne put it: "A people is not really a people and certainly does not live in freedom unless the natural social groups which compose it accept each other, and unless the state recognizes their differences and ensures that their interests are represented."[25] This would be true democratic pluralism.

Notably, these new Christian Democrats renounced the patriarchal, paternalistic family system of old Europe. The father-dominated family could not be reconciled with "personalism," they said. Postwar Christian Democrats held that women should enjoy equal civil, legal, and political rights. Yet restoration of the family did mean that control of education should be returned to parents, that motherhood and childhood should enjoy special protection by the state, and that heads of households should receive a "family wage" in order that mothers might be empowered to remain home with their children.[26]

Human rights became a defining Christian Democratic concern, but with a special twist. Where secular views of the French experience relied on an evolutionary understanding of rights, the new movement rooted human rights in the Creation itself, in the natural law. Such rights were "inviolable" and "innate" because their fountainhead was God himself. Bearing a healthy suspicion of the state, Christian Democrats embraced human rights in order to protect "the natural rights of each individual" and of "natural social groups" from the overweening power of government.[27]

Homo Religiosus

Christian Democracy further refined its economic doctrine. The mid-twentieth-century economist in closest sympathy with Christian Democracy may have been Wilhelm Röpke of Switzerland. Röpke rejected the materialism, utilitarianism, and "economism" of the liberal or libertarian economists, persons who had forgotten "that people do not live by cheaper vacuum cleaners alone but by other and higher things which may wither in the shadow of giant industries and monopolies." He derided the "cult of productivity" and the worship of an abstract "standard of living" as disorders of "spiritual perception."

In place of *homo economicus,* he posited *homo religiosus,* or man created in the image of God, as the proper foundation of economic theory. Röpke insisted that the first "precept of ethical and humane behavior, no less than of political wisdom," is "to adapt economic policy to man, not man to economic policy." Revealing his agrarian sympathies, Röpke accused modern urban-industrial society of being "a breeding ground for god-lessness and animalism." In contrast, the "countryman, whose work is dictated by the changing seasons and is dependent on the elements, feels himself to be a creature of the Almighty." Recalling the libertarian economist who, on observing a sub-urban family at work in their garden, had commented, "this is not a rational way of producing vegetables," Röpke replied that "it may be an eminently rational way of producing happiness, which alone matters in the last resort."[28]

All the same, Röpke firmly defended private property and free markets. Like the English Distributists and the East Euro-pean agrarians before him, Röpke praised ownership as both a "delimitation of the individual sphere of decision and respon-sibility" and a vital "protection of the individual sphere from political power." Widespread ownership means family indepen-dence and liberty; it stands in contrast to monopoly, deemed "economically questionable and morally . . . reprehensible." For their part, "free prices and markets" deserve praise as "the only economic order compatible with human freedom." While the truly "vital things" are "beyond supply and demand and the world of property," Röpke insisted that these latter principles remain the only means of reconciling the necessary task of win-ning one's daily bread with human liberty.[29]

The broad social-political problem, in Röpke's view, is that the market economy requires "a definite spiritual and moral setting" and "ethical reserves" in order to operate; however, "the market, competition, and the play of supply and demand . . . consume them." The virtues on which the system de-pends—"self discipline, a sense of justice, honesty, fairness, chivalry, moderation, public spirit, respect for human dignity, firm ethical norms"—are born outside the market system. They are the products of "[f]amily, church, genuine communities, and tradition," social forces that must operate independently of the marketplace. As Röpke explains:

It is surely the mark of a sound society that the center of gravity of decision and responsibility lies midway between the two extremes of individual and state, within genuine and small communities, of which the most indispensable, primary, and natural is the family. And surely *it is our task to encourage the development of the great variety of small and medium communities* and thereby of group assistance within circles which still have room for voluntary action, a sense of responsibility, and human contact.[30]

This effort to reinvigorate the family and other mediating institutions reveals the cautious Christian Democratic pose toward the welfare state. On the one hand, as Röpke phrases it, "We cannot, nowadays, do without a certain minimum of compulsory state institutions for social security. Public old-age pensions, health insurance, widows' benefits, unemployment relief—there must naturally be room for all of these in . . . a sound social security system in a free society." The guiding principles, however, must be that these programs not redistribute income in an aggressively egalitarian way and that they not undermine voluntary efforts at self-help. Röpke sees the American and Swiss systems of the 1950s—modest in scale and cost—as exemplary in these regards. In addition, Röpke insists that such programs should be structured to augment responsibility and thrift, "as well as the natural solidarity of small groups, above all the family."[31]

Ideals and Results

Out of this genuine intellectual ferment, Christian Democracy took political form in France as the Mouvement Republicain Populaire (MRP), which became part of the French governing coalition of 1946.[32] In the Netherlands, the Anti-Revolutionary

Party, in alliance with the Catholic Party, reclaimed governing power the same year. Christian Democratic parties then won important elections in formerly fascist Italy (1948) and West Germany (1949).[33]

The effect was large. Christian Democracy created the spiritual and political conditions that made possible rapid European economic renewal. It also laid the foundations for the building of welfare states that were broadly supportive of families organized on the male breadwinner–female homemaker, child–rich model. This Christian Democratic moment had two other important results. First, the dream of European Union was largely born among the postwar generation of Christian Democratic leaders, notably Robert Schumann of France, Konrad Adenauer of West Germany, and Alcide de Gaspari of Italy. The early treaties creating the European Coal and Steel Community (Paris, 1952) and the European Economic Community (Rome, 1957) focused ostensibly on economic questions. But their animating spirit came from a dream to revive Christendom; indeed, to build a democratic version of the old Holy Roman Empire on the ruins of a continent recently ravaged by war.

The other enduring legacy of postwar Christian Democracy was the Universal Declaration of Human Rights, adopted by the United Nations General Assembly on December 10, 1948. The key architects of this document were Charles Malik, an Arab Christian Democrat from Lebanon, who served in 1948 both as secretary of the Commission on Human Rights and as president of the UN's Economic and Social Council; and René Cassin, a French specialist in international law who, while himself Jewish, was highly sympathetic toward postwar Christian Democracy.[34] As one historian has phrased it, the Universal Declaration of Human Rights is "largely identical" with the worldview expressed in Christian Democracy.[35]

Specifically, we find in Article 16(3) the affirmation of "natural" social institutions: "The family is the natural and fundamental group unit of society and is entitled to protection by society and the state." The word "natural" comes straight out of the Christian Democratic lexicon. Even the use of the word "society" here as distinct from and prior to "the state" is a Christian Democratic marker.

In Article 25, one finds support for family social rights, with particular emphasis on a "family wage":

> Everyone has the right to a standard of living adequate for the health and well-being of himself and his family, including food, clothing, housing, and medical care and necessary social services, and the right to security in the event of unemployment, sickness, disability, widowhood, old age or other lack of livelihood in circumstances beyond his control.

Other provisions declare that men and women have "the right to marry and found a family" (Article 16[1]) and that "motherhood and childhood are entitled to special care and assistance" (Article 25[2]). The Universal Declaration also affirms parental rights: "Parents have a prior right to choose the kind of education that shall be given to their children" (Article 26[3]).

Even the term "equality," tool before and later of so much mischief, finds rich meaning in the Universal Declaration through "personalist" conceptions of "the right to life" (Article 3), "the dignity and worth of the human person" (Preamble), and "endowed" human nature: "All human beings are born free and equal in dignity and rights. They are endowed with reason and conscience and should act toward one another in a spirit of brotherhood" (Article 1).

The only core Christian Democratic theme not present is an open affirmation of the Deity of Creation. Several members of the drafting committee, led by Charles Malik, attempted to include this idea. But in the end, they agreed to more universal language that implied, rather than named, God.[36]

Silent Revolution

As early as the 1950s, Christian Democracy as a vital world-view entered another period of crisis. The youthful excitement, energy, and sense of positive Christian revolution evident in the 1940s dissipated. In France, Christian Democracy's main political vehicle, the MRP, lost support to General Charles de Gaulle's new party, the RPI (Rassemblement du peuple français), and by 1958 had disappeared altogether. In Italy and West Germany, Christian Democratic parties consolidated their hold on power at the price of their vision. By the early 1960s, they were increasingly pragmatic and bureaucratic, self-satisfied defenders of the status quo. Ambitious office seekers, rather than Christian idealists, came to dominate the parties. Movements for "moral and political renewal" became simply mass parties of the right-of-center.[37] When a new "crisis of values" hit Europe with particular force in the late 1960s, the Christian Democrats were unprepared to respond. They appeared by then to be old and discredited guardians of a new kind of materialism, the very opposite of what the movement's visionaries had intended.[38]

It is now clear that a silent revolution set in among Europeans about 1965. It can be seen in the shift away from values affirmed by Christian teaching (such as "responsibility, sacrifice, altruism, and sanctity of long-term commitments") and toward a strong "secular individualism" focused on the desires of the self.[39] Family life became a casualty. Surveys of European youth in the 1970s and 1980s showed that they "appear to be extending non-conformism with respect to abortion, divorce, etc., to parenthood as well," agreeing by large majorities with statements such as "children need only one parent" and "children are no longer needed for personal fulfillment."

In explaining this value change, another commentator has pointed to the swift legalization of abortion and to "the falling awareness" among Europeans "of the dignity of every person, even the old and disabled." He adds: "naked individualism and unbridled libertinism have become increasingly widespread in recent years. . . . Female emancipation, which is well advanced, . . . appears to be headed in this direction." Meanwhile, the courts and public opinion grew tolerant of sexual deviance.[40] Such changes symbolized the new triumph of an old foe—"the anti-Christian world power" originally unleashed in 1789—over Christian Democracy.

New Hope From the East?

By the 1990s, Christian Democracy, though nearly dead in its native Western Europe, had become resurgent in unexpected places. For instance, a Swedish election in 1991 brought the Christian Democratic Social Party into Sweden's parliament for the first time, where it joined the governing coalition. Over the next three years, the party successfully pushed for the teaching of Christian values in the state schools and for a new social benefit to go to stay-at-home parents.

More dramatically, Christian Democratic parties emerged in all of the East European nations freed from communism in 1989–90. In Poland, to choose one example, the Solidarity Electoral Action bloc came to power in 1997, with a campaign manifesto declaring: "We can build a modern, just, and self-sustaining sovereign state; a state founded on patriotic and Christian values, on love and freedom. These values have formed our core identity for a thousand years." In Romania, the National Peasants' Christian Democratic Party won that nation's November 1996 election. Christian Democratic parties have also been part of ruling coalitions in Hungary, Slovakia, Croatia, the Czech Republic, Lithuania, and Latvia.[41]

Family issues loom large in these nations and on Christian Democratic agendas. The legacy of communism has combined with the arrival of Western-style social libertarianism to produce a devastating effect on East European family structures. Since 1990, divorce rates have soared; marriage rates have fallen sharply; birthrates have plummeted. In 2005, the list of the ten nations with the world's lowest total fertility rates included Latvia (1.26), Poland (1.24), Slovenia (1.24), the Czech Republic (1.20) and Lithuania (1.19). In response, Christian Democratic parliamentarians from six "new member states of the European Union"—namely the Czech Republic, Slovakia, Latvia, Poland, Lithuania, and Estonia—met in 2005 and issued their "Family First Declaration." They formally endorsed the March 2004 "Mexico City Declaration" of the World Congress of Families, and they pledged:

> We will coordinate our efforts on behalf of the traditional family, marriage and the intrinsic value of each human life so that the future Europe is not associated any longer with the culture of death, institutionalized egoism and population decline, but with the preservation of religious, ethical and cultural values that enhance virtuous life in all relevant aspects. Healthy family life enhances true and ordered liberty and limits the power of the state.

This document endorsed other principles central to the Christian Democratic worldview, including:

- "Procreation is the key to the survival of the human race";
- "Parents possess the primary authority and responsibility to direct the upbringing and education of their children";
- "Good government protects and supports the family and does not usurp the vital roles it plays in society"; and
- "Sexuality exists for the expression of love between husband and wife and for the procreation of children in the covenant of marriage."

If Eastern Europe—indeed, if Europe as a whole—has any viable future, it probably lies along these Christian Democratic lines.

Lessons for America

There has never been a serious Christian Democratic party in America. This seems due, in part, to the mechanics of our single-district electoral structure, which strongly favor a two-party system, with each party in turn serving as an ad hoc coalition of interest groups. Christian Democratic parties—with their more coherent worldview—thrive best in places that use proportional representation.

Also, Americans have had a more complex, or one might say confused, relationship with the legacy of the French Revolution. During the 1790s, Americans were more likely to sympathize with the revolution's repudiation of royal and feudal power and its appeals to democracy than to worry about its suppression of the Catholic Church. In 1803, President Thomas Jefferson cut a sweet deal with Napoleon for the purchase of the Louisiana Territory. And in 1812, the United States found itself again at war with France's chief enemy, the British Empire: and the enemy of my enemy is my friend. Relatively few Americans have shared, say, Abraham Kuyper's nightmarish view of "the catastrophe of 1789."

Still, Europe's twentieth-century experiment in Christian Democracy offers several broad lessons for all believers engaged in modern politics:

First, the movement has had the most success when it has stayed true to the "full" Gospel, particularly to Christ's radical command that we love our neighbors as ourselves. Issues of social welfare and social justice lie near the heart of true Christian Democracy.

Second, this movement successfully pioneered ways to funnel public health, education, and welfare programs through churches and church-related agencies, models that should be of interest to a nation now experimenting with faith-based initiatives.

Third, Christian Democracy has, at its best, carved out a Third Way of social-economic policy, independent of both the liberal-capitalist and socialist mindsets, by being respectful of family life and the health of local communities.

And finally, this movement succeeded only so long as it found animation in authentic Christian faith and enthusiasm. When those diminished, so did the coherence and effectiveness of Christian Democracy, and of the modern European nations as a whole.

Conclusion:

Dreams, Realities, Illusions

This recounting of Third Way episodes over the course of the twentieth century might appear, in the end, to be a collective tale of incompleteness, failure, and woe. Dreams of escaping a choice between capitalism and communism seemed to dissipate when faced with the hard realities of economics and politics. What are the actual lessons to be learned from this experience? How can they help us build and maintain a humane culture of enterprise, a free and ordered society conducive to creativity, economic growth, and human happiness?

The Driving Force

To begin with, all the architects of these systems acknowledged—tacitly or openly—that dynamic capitalism was the driving force in the modern world, the social and political touchstone of the age. Even historical diagnostician Karl Polanyi readily acknowledged that capitalism had delivered "a prosperity of gigantic portions . . . for the whole of humankind" and provoked a deep transformation in human affairs.

Alongside the real energy of capitalism, communism was a puny half-experiment. Alexander Chayanov also made important admissions. While analyzing and urging on a modern, co-operative peasant economy, he admitted the need for capitalists with "shark-like propensities," lest the favored cooperators fall into "technical stagnation." Moreover, Chayanov's advocacy of mammoth cooperatives in Russia was undertaken under the shadow of his worry that twentieth-century capitalism would be a much more vigorous force than had been its nineteenth-century ancestor.

At certain times and in certain places it was the advocates of a Third Way who actually came closest to being the "classical liberal," pro-market players in the field. For example, during the 1920s and 1930s, all of the major British political parties favored expanding the nascent welfare state: the Labour Party for reasons of socialist principle; the Tories as a paternalistic measure of social peace; and the Liberals to save capitalism from a worse revolution. Only the Distributists, under the lead of Hilaire Belloc and G. K. Chesterton, warned that measures such as unemployment insurance, a minimum wage, and national health insurance constituted a dangerous new form of servitude. In Russia, Chayanov's quest for a nation of propertied peasants, vital cooperatives, and small-scale capitalism was the only practical alternative in the 1920s to the hypercentralization of the Bolsheviks. He saw a way to respond to the real grievances behind the revolution without descending into inhumanity. In Eastern Europe, where fascists, Communists, and mercantilists conspired to restrict markets, it was the agrarian leader Alexander Stamboliski who pressed for an end to state subsidies of industry and for the building of a Danubian free-trade zone. It was the agrarian economist Virgil Madgearu of Romania who successfully pushed through reduced tariffs on manufactured goods and opened his nation to foreign capital investment. As Polanyi observed, the fierce agrarianism of the postwar years saw the peasants become "the champions of market economy."[1] All of these peasant democracies were, relatively speaking, also "anti-tax."

These Third Way experiments can be seen as answers to common challenges: How might economic development be channeled so as to shelter vital social relations?" What culture might be formed that would nurture enterprise while protecting natural institutions such as the family from commodification? Four answers emerged. Belloc and Chesteron along with the European agrarians favored the broad restoration of property, arguing that the ownership of productive land and capital protected primal family relations and the home economy. American labor leaders, maternalist reformers, the Swedish housewives, and Christian Democrats turned to the family-wage regime. This intentional distortion of the labor market preserved the home as an independent economic unit; treated the important work of women as outside the market's sphere; and kept income redistribution between workers and dependents a family responsibility. Chayanov placed his emphasis on cooperatives. They would allow the "natural family economy" grounded in biological relations to survive within a process of broad economic modernization. Polanyi, for his part, looked to the "always embedded marketplace," or the regulatory state, as the mechanism to protect families and neighborhoods. This process would aim for justice (that is, fairness between persons of different status), a degree of self-sufficiency, and home autonomy.

These experiments were not empty efforts. It is important to remember that they delivered real results: many in the short run; a few on a lasting basis. Over the long haul, Distributist-inspired policies giving direct and indirect subsidies to home ownership became public policy during the 1930s and '40s in the United States, Great Britain, and Australia and remain so to this day. Chayanov was the dominant—and very much an anti-

Bolshevik—voice in Russian agricultural policymaking during the 1920s. Peasant parties implementing Third Way agendas came to power in Czechoslovakia, Bulgaria, Poland, Romania, and other Eastern European lands. They enacted land reforms and launched schemes to modernize the countryside while retaining family-scale economies. Between 1900 and 1970, the family-wage principle successfully reshaped labor markets to protect family bonds in the United States, Canada, Australia, and much of Western Europe. Even in Sweden, the same system undergirded "the golden age" of the socialist housewife. These family-wage projects contributed to a growing equality of households, in America as much as in Sweden. Middle classes grew, while the ranks of the poor and the very rich shrank. Christian Democracy had a decisive influence on European reconstruction after World War II, stimulating the renewal of both national economies and family life on a war-ravaged continent. This movement also inspired the Universal Declaration of Human Rights and the successful dream of European Union.

Naïve Decency, Intellectual Weariness

Most of these schemes failed in the end. Part of the reason lay in the relative decency of Third Way advocates in an era dominated by violence and moral monsters. Chayanov actually believed that the Russian Revolution was about intellectual freedom and democracy, as well as economic justice. His writing anticipates that the Bolsheviks would respect non-Marxist plans implemented on behalf of the solid peasant majority. He failed to anticipate the rise and brutality of Stalin. Peasant leaders in Eastern Europe also placed their faith in democracy and constitutional governance. With actual or near majorities, they believed that the democratic revolutions of 1918 justly gave them the opportunity to rule and to pursue policies favoring family-scale agriculture. Alas, their enemies—Communists, fascists, militarists, hypernationalists, racists, royalitists, and monopolists—were more ruthless, ready to suppress democracy and murder peasant leaders and others who stood in their way. Only Stamboliski seemed to understand the real peril here; his volunteer Orange Guard was the sort of formation needed to protect peasant democracy. But even it failed to prevent his overthrow, torture, and execution. Rivals also slayed Stephan Radic in Croatia, while military or fascist coups crushed peasant governments in Poland and Romania. The innate decency of the Swedish socialist housewives as child- and home-centered women allowed them to fall victim to the social-engineering schemes of a hard-left regime. Correctly labelled the era of "Red Sweden,"[2] the first Olaf Palme government committed a kind of feminist genocide, intentionally eliminating a whole class of women through coerced "reeducation" and forced labor.

All of these Third Way architects faced the same dilemma: In the face of coercive violence, do we hold to our ideals and so fail? Or do we bend democracy and abandon nonviolence in order—they hoped—to save both in the long run? The first question was usually answered "yes," with tragic results.

Several of these schemes collapsed because they lost vital energy and a sustaining intellectual matrix. In the United States, when equity feminists during the 1960s mounted a new challenge to the family-wage regime, there were relatively few vocal defenders of the old order. The great army of maternalist writers and advocates and their labor-union counterparts were retired or dead, and they left few heirs. In his controversial 1965 report on "the Negro American Family," labor analyst Daniel Patrick Moynihan did see the strengthening of bread-winner–homemaker families as the best solution to growing poverty among African Americans. However, he was quickly silenced by the new cultural relativists.[3] A few years later, Phyllis Schlafly and her Eagles rose in defense of the full-time mother and homemaker in the context of their campaign against the

Equal Rights Amendment. Although they successfully quashed the ERA, they failed to save the apparatus of the family-wage system from the regulators in the Equal Employment Opportunity Commission.[4]

In the Sweden of that era, there was also an intellectual vacuum. Nancy Eriksson's *Only a Housewife* was the lone book to appear in defense of the old Third Way. Even though the great majority of young Swedish mothers were housewives in the mid-1960s and apparently content to remain so, public defenders of the system were almost exclusively older women. Among the Christian Democrats on the continent, the religiously infused idealism of the 1940s gave way to the practical politics of right-of-center political coalition-building. This meant compromises with both state bureaucracies and the great corporations. A movement originally opposed to economic materialism of both the socialist-Communist and liberal-capitalistic sorts came increasingly to be the servant of gross national products.

Who Won?

By the 1990s, the search for a Third Way economy was over. One reason was that the "Second Way" of communism had dissolved around the globe. The collapse of the Soviet Union in 1991 and the spread of economic liberalism into the People's Republic of China seemed to bring an end to the greater contest between capitalism and communism. With only one of the mega-combatants still standing, the quest for a Third Way became illogical.

Indeed, from the fall of the Berlin Wall in 1989 until the global financial crisis of 1997, there was a broad consensus about the triumph of the market economy in nearly every important nation. These years, in economist Joseph Stiglitz's words, were "[t]he heyday of neoliberal doctrine."[5]

Yet other historical currents were already in motion. As Stiglitz notes, among the developed Western nations neoliberal concepts were actually in retreat during these years: "this period was marked almost everywhere by a rejection of these doctrines, the Reagan-Thatcher free market doctrines, in favor of 'New Democrat' or 'New Labor' policies."[6] Since 2000, most Latin American nations have abandoned neoliberal market systems, opting instead for various forms of mercantilism or populist socialism. Moreover, international-trade liberalization through the Doha Round has come to a halt.[7]

So if communism is discredited intellectually and shattered beyond repair, and if free-market neoliberalism is in broad retreat, who really won the great ideological contest of the twentieth century? Perhaps the real winner was that phantom entity first identified by Hilaire Belloc nearly a century ago: the Servile State. Recall the Englishman's explanation of its origins: "the effect of socialist doctrine upon capitalist society is to produce a third thing different from either of its two begetters." He defines this "stable equilibrium" as one involving "compulsory labor legally enforceable upon those who do not own the means of production for the advantage of those who do." Owners accept certain paternalistic obligations toward workers, commonly mediated through the state; workers accept their servile status in exchange for security.

Where might we see signs of the contemporary Servile State? To begin with, the reality of private property may be dimming, with its vital qualities being replaced by state benefits. As early as 1969, Sweden's justice minister premised a basic reform of Sweden's marriage laws on declining public interest in material property in favor of pensions, annuities, and other claims on the welfare state.[8] A recent report by the American Land Foundation finds a troubling tendency by American courts "to transfer individual property rights as envisioned by the Founding Fathers to the government and its right to promote the public good," a concept defined through Jean-Jacques Rousseau's purported "General Will."[9] Curiously, even the seemingly benign and ubiquitous new institution called neighborhood or homeowner associations may be corrupting private property. In one analyst's words, these quasi-governmental associations using restrictive covenants on homes are far more "arbitrary, unresponsive, and dictatorial" than zoning boards in exercising control over private activities. Apropos families, they are especially hostile to home businesses, vegetable gardens, and other forms of production for use.[10]

Another sign of the Servile State is the strange new subjection of women. As noted in chapter 2, the brave new world of the twenty-first-century American corporation demands the deeper integration of women—all women—into the labor force. Being "more skilled" in the needed new challenges of handling ambiguity and building networks, women are to be freed from child- and elder-care; properly refitted men should take their places as part of the "workplace revolution." Meanwhile, poor single mothers are to be moved out of their homes into minimum-wage work, with their children placed in collective care. Two advocates for the revolution praise Hillary Clinton's book *It Takes A Village* and explain, "each of us—society as a whole—bears responsibility for all children, even other people's children"; this is merely another summons to build the postfamilial welfare state.[11]

In Sweden, the same end has been achieved through the open nationalization of women's work. Most Swedish women still perform childcare, teaching, eldercare, and social service, but they now do so as specialists working for the state. Traditional women's tasks have become the "loathsome thing called Social Service," the phrase coined by G. K. Chesterton.

And Sweden has aggressively exported this system into the European Union and beyond. As a 2004 government statement on "EU Policy" explains: "Sweden has a particular responsibility for increasing the pace of gender equality efforts in Europe."[12] This Swedish model involves "an individualization of rights," a "new gender balance in working life," and "changes in family structure" to eliminate the breadwinner and his housewife.[13] EU leaders in turn have pushed these views on recalcitrant member states such as Poland, Latvia, and Croatia. A recent OECD (Organization for Economic Cooperation and Development) report praises Sweden's coercion of women with small children into the labor force. Indeed, it even recommends that the Swedish government make greater use of young mothers in state jobs, since they come relatively cheap.[14]

A third sign of the Servile State as winner comes from Russia, where Chayanov's dream of a family-centered peasant economy died three-quarters of a century ago. Today, in the early twenty-first century, "Mafia capitalism" has clearly won in Russia, beating out both communism and market liberalism. Property is highly concentrated among a small group of owners who proudly call themselves oligarchs. A minimalist welfare state inherited from the Communist era keeps the large majority of the population alive (although working-class men commonly drink themselves to early deaths). Cash enters the system through mercantilist control over oil. These traits are almost pure expressions of Belloc's pleasant nightmare.

Although the new slavery of the Servile State may be most visible in Russia, it is probably most thorough and complete in lands following the Swedish model. In America, residual attachments to property ownership seem to have slowed the process of transformation. All the same, Americans are moving toward the same end, seen in the high proportion of working women (over 70 percent) to be found in state health, education, welfare, and childcare networks. The new slavery triumphs, just as the Chesterbelloc predicted. Rather than enterprise, it promotes and treasures predictability. Rather than liberty, it aims toward security. The newly enslaved are allowed the illusions of freedom and independence—illusions nurtured by a popular culture promising sexual delights. This marks the cruel genius of the triumphant Servile State.

The Family Way

In terms of political economy, there now seems to be only one big player, not two. It may be called the Servile State; or the "Business Government" of Chesterton; or the "State Capitalism" of modern parlance. Belloc thought that this system would be highly stable, resistant to change. However, those who still seek an authentic liberty premised on personal autonomy, family integrity, and a culture of enterprise might still look to the Third Way tradition to find the shape of a fresh alternative. It might now be called the Second Way or—perhaps more accurately—the Family Way. Phrased positively, this model would:

1. *Treasure private property as the foundation of a free society.* The Distributists, the agrarians, and the housewives and their mates understood that liberty requires a material foundation in land, home, and other real property, and that a true democracy puts such property in the grasp of nearly all its citizens. While mutual funds, stock certificates, and bonds are also valued forms of ownership, they can never confer the autonomy offered by *real* or physical property.

2. *Understand that the central social and political challenge is to keep competition and the quest for efficiency out of the family and the local community, and at the same time to keep altruism out of central governments.* Almost all the cultural devices, laws, and regulations devised by the architects of Third Ways ultimately had two purposes: (1) to protect the altruism rooted in self-denial that defines the healthy bonds of wife to husband, parent to child, neighbor to neighbor, and generation to generation; and (2) to prevent the application of the same altruism to the nation-state, where it would quickly descend into the confusion

and coercion of socialism. Put another way, a barrier must stand between the vital principles of the natural home economy and the dynamic operations of the larger market economy, lest both fall into ruin.

3. *Defend the natural family economy through appeals to human biology and human history.* Efforts in Sweden, America, and elsewhere to justify the autonomous home as more efficient or more scientific rested on a fatal error. Its advocates adopted a form of social and economic accounting unsuited to the dynamics of the home. The real family economy, as Chayanov explains, rests on the cooperation of the married couple and, more importantly, on the generation of children. History teaches that every healthy and sustainable culture builds on the biological triad of mother-father-offspring and jealously protects its integrity.

4. *Place primary faith in cultural affirmations and defenses, and only secondary trust in state actions.* Family-wage systems worked best when they were woven into a normative fabric of assumptions about the integrity of the home, the complementarity of men and women, and the needs of children. They were clumsiest when they relied on wages fixed by government. They were most at risk when blended into social-welfare benefits. Agrarian cultures functioned best when the farmer preferred to have his neighbor, rather than his neighbor's land. They were imperiled when such choices had to be imposed by the state.

5. *Attempt to infuse religious energy into culture, politics, and economic life as the surest source of renewal.* Secular campaigns on behalf of the family economy are unlikely to disturb the equilibrium of the Servile State. Only *homo religiosus*, Wilhelm Röpke's name for man created in the image of God, can stand up to the servile heir of *homo economicus*. Even then, the members of each new generation must receive or otherwise acquire that form of enthusiasm and conviction, lest they falter, like Europe's Christian Democrats in the 1960s.

6. *Build on small acts.* In the end, the Family Way means re-connecting everyday tasks with the great purposes of the Creator. Only then do common deeds bend toward transcendence. As the contemporary American agrarian Wendell Berry states, "it may be that our marriages, kinships, friendships, neighborhoods, and all our forms and acts of homemaking are the rites by which we solemnize and enact our union with the universe."[15] In this manner, the Family Way offers a way, perhaps, to overcome much of our alienation, to reconcile humankind with its created nature, to bring about a simple and yet profound coming home.

Notes

1. "Chesterbelloc" and the Fairy Tale of Distributism

1. Michael Mason, "Chesterbelloc," in D. J. Conlon, ed., *G. K. Chesterton: A Half Century of Views* (Oxford and New York: Oxford University Press, 1987), 241.

2. Michael Coren, *Gilbert: The Man Who Was G. K. Chesterton* (London: Jonathan Cape, 1989), 235–36, 246.

3. Ian Boyd, "Chesterton and Distributism," in Conlon, *G. K. Chesterton*, 285.

4. Quoted in Ibid., 286.

5. Joseph Pearce, *Old Thunder: A Life of Hilaire Belloc* (New York: Harper Collins, 2002), 195.

6. A. N. Wilson, *Hilaire Belloc* (London: Hamish Hamilton, 1984), 294.

7. Dudley Barker, *G. K. Chesterton: A Biography* (New York: Stein and Day, 1973), 258.

8. Margaret Canovan, *G. K. Chesterton: Radical Populist* (New York and London: Harcourt Brace Jovanovich, 1977), 93.

9. Brocard Sewell, "Devereux Nights: A Distributist Memoir," in John Sullivan, ed., *G. K. Chesterton: A Centenary Appraisal* (London: Paul Elek, 1974), 142, 145.

10. Boyd, "Chesterton and Distributism," 286.

11. John Carey, "For Beer and Liberty," in Conlon, *G. K. Chesterton*, 346.

12. Mason, "Chesterbelloc," 243.

13. Canovan, *G. K. Chesterton*, 89.

14. Coren, *Gilbert*, 237.

15. Kinley E. Roby, ed., *Hilaire Belloc* (Boston, MA: G. K. Hall and Company, 1982), 126–27.

16. Robert Speaight, *The Life of Hilaire Belloc* (London: Hollis & Carter, 1957), 318.

17. Noted in Barker, *G. K. Chesterton*, 276.

18. Ibid., 242.

19. Open letter from Chesterton to Belloc in the *New Witness*, April 27, 1923; quoted in Pearce, *Old Thunder*, 196.

20. John P. McCarthy, *Hilaire Belloc: Edwardian Radical* (Indianapolis, IN: Liberty Press, 1978), 273.

21. Christopher Hollis, *The Mind of Chesterton* (London: Hollis & Carter, 1970), 15.

22. Coren, *Gilbert*, 239.

23. "Forty Years On," *G. K.'s Weekly* 13 (May 23, 1931): 1.

24. Quoted in Michael Ffinch, *G. K. Chesterton* (New York: Harper & Row, 1986), 305. Emphasis added.

25. Coren, *Gilbert*, 234; emphasis added.

26. *Rerum Novarum: The Encyclical of Pope Leo XIII on Capital and Labor*, given 15 May 1891; at http://www.vatican.va/holy_father/leo_xiii/encyclicals/documents/hf_1-xiii_enc_1505189 (11/27/2006): 2, 4.

27. Ibid., 3.

28. Ibid., 4.

29. Ibid., 12, 14–15. Emphasis added.

30. See: Boyd, "Chesterton and Distributism," 284; and McCarthy, *Hilaire Belloc*, 300.

31. Quoted in McCarthy, *Hilaire Belloc*, 284. See: H. G. Wells, *New Worlds for Old* (New York: Macmillan, 1907); George Bernard Shaw, *Man and Superman* (Harmondsworth, UK: Penguin Books, 1946 [1903]); and Sidney and Beatrice Webb, *The Prevention of Destitution* (London: Longmans, Green, 1911).

32. Canovan, *G. K. Chesterton*, 80.

33. Maisie Ward, *Gilbert Keith Chesterton* (New York: Sheed and Ward, 1943), 513–14.

34. Canovan, *G. K. Chesterton*, 82; Boyd, "Chesterton and Distributism," 284; and Hollis, *The Mind of Chesterton*, 117.

35. Reprinted in: D. J. Conlon, ed., *G. K. Chesterton: Critical Judgments Part 1: 1900–1937* (Antwerp, Belgium: Antwerp Studies in English Literature, 1976), 248.

36. G. K. Chesterton, *What's Wrong With the World*, in George J. Marlin, Richard P. Rabatin, and John L. Swan, eds., *The Collected Work of G. K. Chesterton*, vol. 4 (San Francisco: Ignatius Press, 1987), 65–67.

37. Ibid., 68–69.

38. Ibid., 77–88, 71.

39. Ibid., 72–73. Emphasis added.

40. Ibid., 65–66.

41. Hilaire Belloc, *The Servile State* (Indianapolis, IN: Liberty Classics, 1977 [1912/13]), 39.

42. Ibid., 32, 35.

43. Ibid., 49–50, 61.

44. R. H. Tawney, *The Agrarian Problem in the Sixteenth Century* (London: Longmans, Green, 1912); an influence reported in McCarthy, *Hilaire Belloc*, 296.

45. Belloc, *The Servile State*, 64–81, 87.

46. Ibid., 82–104.

47. Ibid., 107–18. Inaugurated in 1795, the Speenhamland system had parishes pay an allowance to day laborers based on the number of their children.

48. Ibid., 122–52.

49. This is the interpretation that sociologist Robert Nisbet provides in his introduction to the Liberty Press edition of *The Servile State*; see ibid., 13–23.

50. See McCarthy, *Hilaire Belloc*, 301–2.

51. Belloc, *The Servile State*, 174–93.

52. Ibid., 198.

53. Ibid., 131–33.

54. Hilaire Belloc, "Reform: IV—Restoration of Property in Capital," *Oxford and Cambridge Review* 25 (Nov. 1912): 87–96.

55. Hilaire Belloc, "Reform: III—The Restoration of Property," *Oxford and Cambridge Review* 24 (Oct. 1912): 65. Emphasis added.

56. Ward, *Gilbert Keith Chesterton*, 518.

57. G. K. Chesterton, *The Outline of Sanity* (Norfolk, VA: IHS Press, 2001), 26–28, 182.

58. Ibid., 29–30, 34, 70.

59. Ibid., 34–36, 62.

60. Ibid., 41–43, 55–56.

61. Ibid., 87–88.

62. Ibid., 52, 64, 76, 89.

63. The Limehouse project was an early-twentieth-century English experiment in "urban renewal" that involved the elimination of tenements, with their irregular yards and gardens, and their replacement with modernist high-rises.

64. Chesterton, *The Outline of Sanity*, 78–79, 94, 104, 107–9, 125, 142–45.

65. Ibid., 173–74.

66. Hilaire Belloc, *The Restoration of Property* (New York: Sheed & Ward, 1936), 10, 12.

67. Pearce, *Old Thunder*, 195.

68. McCarthy, *Hilaire Belloc*, 310.

69. Belloc, *The Restoration of Property*, 135, 144.

70. Ibid., 14–17.

71. Ibid., 18–19, 29–30, 35, 37–38.

72. Ibid., 44–45, 56, 58.

73. Ibid., 68–70, 72, 77, 85–86, 93, 96, 106–7, 109, 113–17, 139, 141–43.

74. Ibid., 119–30.

75. Wilson, *Hilaire Belloc*, 294.

76. "Hitler as Distributist," *G. K.'s Weekly* 17 (June 8, 1933): 1–2.

77. "Unemployment: A Distributist Solution," *G. K.'s Weekly* 7 (June 23, 1928): 228.

78. H. S. D. Went, "The Drink Problem: A Distributist Solution," *G. K.'s Weekly* 11 (Feb. 22, 1930): 373.

79. An incident reported in Speaight, *The Life of Hilaire Belloc*, 486.

80. Sewell, "Devereux Nights," 153–55.

81. Winston S. Churchill, "Speech to Conservative Party Conference, October 5, 1946," at http://www.fordham.edu/halsall/mod/1946churchill-conservatism.html (12/5/2006): 1–2. Emphasis added.

82. Anthony Eden, "United for Peace and Progress"; British Conservative Party Election Manifesto, 1955; at http://www.psr.keele.ac.uk/area/uk-man/con55.htm (12/5/2006): 2.

83. "Are You Thinking What We're Thinking? It's Time for Action: Conservative Election Manifesto 2005"; at http://www.conservatives.com/tile.do?def-manifesto.uk.accountability.page (12/5/2006): 2.

84. Herbert Agar, "The Task for Conservatism," *American Review* 3 (April 1934): 1–16.

85. See Herbert Agar, "Free America," *Free America* 1 (Jan. 1937): 1–2.

86. Noted in the official history of this project; see Russell Lord and Paul H. Johnstone, *A Place on Earth: A Critical Appraisal of Subsistence Homesteads* (Washington, DC: U.S. Department of Agriculture, Bureau of Agricultural Economics, 1942), 6, 12, 14–17, 20.

87. See: Race Matthews, *Jobs of Our Own—Building a Stakeholder Society—Alternatives to the Market and the State* (Sydney: Pluto Press, 1999).

88. B. A. Santamaria, *Against the Tide* (Melbourne: Oxford University Press, 1981); and Peter Hunt, "Chesterton, Distributism and Australia," *Chesterton Review* 24 (August 1998): 287–93.

89. Stewart D. Friedman and Jeffrey H. Greenhaus, *Work and Family: Allies or Enemies? What Happens When Business Professionals Confront Life Choices* (Oxford and New York: Oxford University Press, 2000).

90. Jody Heymann, *The Widening Gap: Why America's Working Families Are in Jeopardy and What Can Be Done About It* (New York: Basic Books, 2000).

91. Theda Skocpol, *The Missing Middle: Working Families and the Future of American Social Policy* (New York: Norton, 2000).

92. For a broader discussion of these themes, see Allan Carlson, "Creative Destruction, Family Style," *Intercollegiate Review* 37 (Spring 2002): 49–57.

93. Ffinch, *G. K. Chesterton*, 305.

2. The Wages of Kin: Building a Secular Family-Wage Regime

1. Adam Smith, *An Inquiry Into the Nature and Causes of the Wealth of Nations* (New York: P. F. Collier & Son, 1911), 72.

2. Adam Smith, *The Theory of Moral Sentiments* (New Rochelle, NY: Arlington House, 1971), 195, 321.

3. Thomas R. Malthus, *The Pamphlets of Thomas Robert Malthus* (New York: Augustus M. Kelley, 1970), 41–43.

4. Letter, Ricardo to Trower, Jan. 26, 1918, in Samuel Hollander, *The Economics of David Ricardo* (Toronto: University of Toronto Press, 1979), 577.

5. Friedrich Engels, *The Condition of the Working Class in England* (New York: Macmillan, 1958), 51–83.

6. Karl Marx, *Capital: The Process of Capitalist Production*, vol. 1 (New York: International Publishers, 1967), 395.

7. Jane Humphries, "Enclosures, Common Rights, and Women: The Proletarianization of Families in the Late Eighteenth and Early Nineteenth Centuries," *Journal of Economic History* 50 (1990): 243–44.

8. Karl Kautsky, *The Class Struggle* (New York: Norton, 1971): 25–26.

9. John Stuart Mill, *Principles of Political Economy* (New York: Augustus M. Kelley, 1961), 399–401.

10. Alfred Marshall, *Principles of Economics*, vol. 1 (New York: Macmillan, 1895), 774.

11. Quoted in P. Hollis, *Class and Conflict in Nineteenth Century England: 1815–1850* (London: Routledge & Kegan Paul, 1973), 193–94.

12. Jane Lewis, *Women in England, 1870–1950: Sexual Divisions and Social Change* (Bloomington, IN: Indiana University Press, 1984), 49.

13. Clementina Black, *Sweated Industry and the Minimum Wage* (London: Duckworth, 1907), 148.

14. L. Chiozza Money, *Riches and Poverty* (London: Methuen, 1905), 169.

15. B. L. Hutchins and A. Harrison, *A History of Factory Legislation* (London: P. S. King & Son, 1903), 198.

16. Ivy Pinchbeck, *Women Workers and the Industrial Revolution, 1750–1850* (London: Virago, 1969), 312.

17. Ruth Milkman, "Organizing the Sexual Division of Labor: Historical Perspectives on 'Women's Work' and the American Labor Movement," *Socialist Review* 49 (Jan./Feb. 1980): 198.

18. Ada Nield Chew, "The Problem of the Married Working Woman," in *Ada Nield Chew* (London: Virago, 1982), 230–33.

19. Harold Benenson, "The 'Family Wage' and Working Women's Consciousness in Britain, 1880–1914," *Politics and Society* 19 (March 1991): 230–39.

20. Michelle Barrett and Mary McIntosh, "The 'Family Wage': Some Problems for Socialists and Feminists," *Capital and Class* II (1980): 56.

21. Eli Zaretsky, "Capitalism, the Family, and Personal Life," *Socialist Revolution* 3 (Jan.–April 1973): 66–125; and (May–June 1973): 19–70.

22. Heidi Hartman, "The Unhappy Marriage of Marxism and Feminism: Toward a More Progressive Union," *Capital and Class* 8 (1979): 1–33.

23. Mimi Abramovitz, *Regulating the Lives of Women: Social Welfare Policy from Colonial Times to the Present* (Boston: South End Press, 1988).

24. Zillah Eisenstein, *Feminism and Sexual Equality: Crisis in Liberal America* (New York: Monthly Review Press, 1984).

25. Zillah Eisenstein, *Capitalist Patriarchy and the Case for Socialist Feminism* (New York: Monthly Review Press, 1979).

26. Henry Ford, *My Life and Work* (Garden City, NY: Doubleday, 1922), 116, 123.

27. Albion Guilford Taylor, "Labor Policies of the National Association of Manufacturers," *University of Illinois Studies in the Social Sciences* 15 (1927): 43. Emphasis added.

28. Ibid., 126–29.

29. Lillian Holmen Mohr, *Frances Perkins* (Croton-on-Hudson, NY: North River Press, 1979), 192; and Mary Anderson and Mary N. Winslow, *Women at Work: The Autobiography of Mary Anderson* (Minneapolis: University of Minnesota Press, 1951), 171.

30. Martha E. May, "Home Life: Progressive Social Reformers' Prescriptions for Social Stability, 1890–1920," Doctoral Dissertation, State University of New York at Binghamton, 1984. *Dissertation Abstracts International*, A45(4), 146–50.

31. Sara Horrell and Jane Humphries, "Class Struggle and the Persistence of the Working Class Family," *Cambridge Journal of Economics* 1 (1977): 256.

32. Alice Kessler-Harris, *A Woman's Wage: Historical Meanings and Social Consequences* (Lexington, KY: The University Press of Kentucky, 1990), 62.

33. Michael J. Piore, *Unemployment and Inflation: Institutional and Structural Views* (New York: Random House, 1979), 6.

34. Carol Pateman, "The Patriarchal Welfare State," in Amy Gutmann, ed., *Democracy in the Welfare State* (Princeton, NJ: Princeton University Press, 1988).

35. Frances F. Piven, "Ideology and the State: Women, Power and the Welfare State," in Linda Gordon, ed., *Women, the State and Welfare* (Madison, WI: University of Wisconsin Press, 1990), 255.

36. Hillary Land, "The Family Wage," *Feminist Review* 6 (1980): 60.

37. George Alter, "Work and Income in the Family Economy: Belgium," *Journal of Interdisciplinary History* 15 (Autumn 1984): 225–76.

38. Kari Skrede, "Familjeokonomi og forsorgerlonn," *Tidsskrift for Samfunns-forskning* 25 (1984): 359–88.

39. Harold Benenson, "The 'Family Wage' and Working Women's Consciousness in Britain," 71.

40. Horrell and Humphries, "Class Struggle and the Persistence of the Working-Class Family," 243–44.

41. Martha E. May, "The Historical Problem of the Family Wage: The Ford Motor Company and the Five Dollar Day," *Feminist Studies* 8 (1978): 403–4.

42. Ruth Milkman, "Organizing the Sexual Division of Labor: Historical Perspectives on 'Women's Work' and the American Labor Movement," *Socialist Review* 49 (Jan./Feb. 1980): 95–150.

43. Barbara Nachtrieh Armstrong, *Insuring the Essentials: Minimum Wage Plus Social Insurance—A Living Wage Program* (New York: Macmillan, 1932), 145–46.

44. Annika Baude and Per Holmberg, "The Positions of Men and Women in the Labour Market," in E. Dahlstrom, ed., *The Changing Roles of Men and Women* (Boston: Beacon, 1971), 106–7.

45. Philip S. Foner, *Women and the American Labor Market: From World War I to the Present* (New York: The Free Press, 1980), 256–58, 353.

46. Ibid., 353–56; and Walter Fogel, *The Equal Pay Act: Implications for Comparable Worth* (New York: Praeger, 1984), 8, 14–15.

47. Victor R. Fuchs, "Differences in Hourly Earnings Between Men and Women," *Monthly Labor Review* 94 (1971): 14.

48. Fuchs, "Differences in Hourly Earnings Between Men and Women," 9–13.

49. J. N. Hedges, "Women Workers and Manpower Demands in the 1970's," *Monthly Labor Review* 93 (1970): 19–29.

50. Vernon T. Clover, *Changes in Differences in Earnings and Occupational Status of Men and Women, 1947–1967* (Lubbock, TX: Department of Economics, Texas Tech University, 1970).

51. United Auto Workers, Women's Department, *Report: 1968 Constitutional Convention* [Pamphlet, 1969–?], 1–2, 9.

52. James J. Kenneally, *Women and American Trade Unions* (St. Albans, VT: Eden Press Women's Publications, 1978), 181–82, 191–99.

53. Claudia Goldin, *Understanding the Gender Gap: An Economic History of American Women* (New York: Oxford University Press, 1990), 201–2.

54. Donald Allen Robinson, "Two Movements in Pursuit of Equal Employment Opportunity," *Signs: Journal of Women in Culture and Society* 4 (no. 3, 1979): 427.

55. J. E. Buckley, "Equal Pay in America," in B. O. Pettiman, ed., *Equal Pay for Women: Progress and Problems in Seven Countries* (Bradford, UK: MCB Books, 1975), 47.

56. Andrea Beller, "Title VII and the Male/Female Earnings Gap: An Economic Analysis," *Harvard University's Women's Law Journal* 1 (1978): 153–73. Emphasis added.

57. Goldin, *Understanding the Gender Gap*, 203–4.

58. U.S. Bureau of the Census, *Statistical Abstract of the United States* (Washington, DC: U.S. Government Printing Office, 1995): Table 738.

59. U.S. Bureau of the Census, *Statistical Abstract of the United States* (Washington, DC: U.S. Government Printing Office, 1994): Tables 732 and 1264.

60. S. A. Holmes, "Low Wage Fathers and the Welfare Debate," *New York Times* (April 25, 1995): A2.

61. Ernst Mandel, *Late Capitalism* (London: LLB, 1975), 391.

62. L. Cornell and J. Karlsson, "Arbetets Sociala Form," *Historisk Tidsskrift* 4 (1983): 393–415.

63. Christopher Lasch, "The Freudian Left and Cultural Revolution," *New Left Review* 129 (1981): 33.

64. Allan Carlson, *From Cottage to Work Station: The Family's Search for Social Harmony in the Industrial Age* (San Francisco: Ignatius, 1993), 139–57; and Susan M. Strasser, *Never Done: A History of Housework* (New York: Pantheon Books, 1982), 240.

65. S. M. Smith, R. Hanson, and S. Noble, "Social Aspects of the Battered Baby Syndrome," in J. V. Cook and R. T. Bowles, eds., *Child Abuse: Commission and Omission* (Toronto: Butterworths, 1980), 205–25; and Martin Daly and Margo Wilson, "Child Abuse and Other Risks of Not Living with Both Parents," *Ethology and Sociobiology* 6 (1985): 197–209.

66. Steven Stack, "The Impact of Divorce on Suicide in Norway, 1951–1980," *Journal of Marriage and the Family* 51 (1989): 229–38; and Steven Stack, "The Effects of Suicide in Denmark, 1961–1980," *Sociological Quarterly* 31 (1990): 361–68.

67. Isador Chein, Donald C. Gerard, Robert S. Lee, and Eva Rosenfeld, *The Road to H: Narcotics, Delinquency, and Social Policy* (New York: Basic Books, 1964); Denise B. Kandel, "Drug and Drinking Behavior Among Youth," *Annual Review of Sociology* 6 (1980): 235–85; Judith S. Brook, Martin Whiteman, and Ann Scovall Gordon, "Stages of Drug Use in Adolescence: Personality, Peer, and Family Correlates," *Developmental Psychology* 19 (1983): 269–88; Kazno Yamaguchi and Denise B. Kandel, "Dynamic Relationships Between Premarital Cohabitation and Illicit Drug Use: An Event-History Analysis of Role Selection and Role Socialization," *American Sociological Review* 50 (1985a): 530–46; and Kazno Yamaguchi and Denise B. Kandel, "On the Resolution of Role Incompatibility: A Life Event History Analysis of Family Rules and Marijuana Use," *American Journal of Sociology* 90 (1985b): 1284–1325.

68. A. J. Beck and S. A. Kline, "Survey of Youth in Custody, 1987," *U.S. Department of Justice, Bureau of Justice Statistics, Special Report* (Washington, DC:

U.S. Department of Justice, September 1988); P. Marquis, " Family Disfunc-
tion as a Risk Factor in the Development of Antisocial Behavior," *Psychological Reports* 71 (1992): 468–70; R. A. Knight and R. A. Prentky, "The Developmental Antecedents and Adult Adaptations of Rapist Subtypes," *Criminal
Justice and Behavior* 14 (1987): 403–26; J. Figueira-McDonough, "Residence,
Dropping Out, and Delinquency Rates," *Deviant Behavior* 14 (1993): 109–
32; and M. A. Pirog-Good, "Teenage Paternity, Child Support, and Crime,"
Social Science Quarterly 69 (1988): 527–47.

69. D. A. Dawson, "Family Structure and Children's Health and Well-Being:
Data From the 1988 National Health Interview Survey on Child Health,"
Paper presented at the Annual Meeting of the Population Association of
America, Toronto (1990); J. C. Kleinman and S. S. Kessel, "Racial Differences in Low Birth Weight," *New England Journal of Medicine* 317 (1987):
749–53; F. Saucier and A. Ambert, "Parental Marital Status and Adolescents'
Health-Risk Behavior," *Adolescence* 18 (1983): 403–11; W. J. Doherty and
R. H. Needle, " Psychological Adjustment and Substance Use Among Adolescents Before and After a Parental Divorce," *Child Development* 62 (1991):
328–37; R. H. Needle, S. S. Su, and W. J. Doherty, "Divorce, Remarriage,
and Adolescent Substance Use: A Prospective Longitudinal Study," *Journal of
Marriage and the Family* 52 (1990): 157–69.

70. C. E. Bowerman and G. H. Elder Jr., "Variations in Adolescent Percep-
tion of Family Power Structure," *American Sociological Review* 29 (1964): 551–
67; Kevin Marjoribanks, "Environment, Social Class, and Mental Abilities,"
Journal of Educational Psychology Reports 63 (1972): 103–9; D. B. Lynn, *The
Father: His Role in Child Development* (Monterey, CA: Brooks/Cole, 1974); B.
Kimball, "The Sentence Completion Technique in the Study of Scholastic
Underachievement," *Journal of Consulting Psychology* 16 (1952): 353–58; H. B.
Biller, *Paternal Deprivation: Family, School, Sexuality, and Society* (Lexington,
MA: Lexington Books, 1974); J. W. Santrock, "Relation of Type and Onset
of Father Absence to Cognitive Development," *Child Development* 43 (1972):
457–69; and R. B. Zajonc, "Family Configuration and Intelligence," *Science*
192 (1976): 227–36.

71. E. S. Kisker and N. Goldman, "Perils of Single Life and Benefits of Marriage," *Social Biology* 34 (1990): 135–52; Y. Hu and N. Goldman, "Mortality
Differentials by Marital Status: An International Comparison," *Demography*
27 (1990): 233–50; A. Rosengren and L. Wilhelmsen, "Marital Status and
Mortality in Middle-Aged Swedish Men," *American Journal of Epidemiology*
129 (1989): 54–63; and O. Anson, "Living Arrangements and Women's
Health," *Social Science and Medicine* 26 (1988): 201–8.

72. J. Lee, "A Redivision of Labour: Victoria's Wage Boards in Action,"
Historical Studies 22 (1987).

73. Henry Bourne Higgins, *A New Province for Law and Order* (London: Con-

stable and Co., 1922); O. R. Foenander, *Towards Industrial Peace in Australia* (Melbourne: Melbourne University Press, 1937); and George Anderson, *Fixation of Wages in Australia* (Melbourne: Macmillan, 1929).

74. Harleigh Hartmann, *Should the State Interfere in the Determination of Wage Rates?* (New York: National Industrial Conference Board, 1920), 65. Emphasis added.

75. *Adkins v. Children's Hospital*, 261 U.S. 525, nos. 795, 796 (October 1922).

76. Eleanor Rathbone, *The Case for Family Allowances* (Harmondsworth, UK: Penguin, 1940).

77. Paul H. Douglas, *Wages and the State* (Chicago: University of Chicago Press, 1925/27).

78. Jane Humphries, "Enclosures, Common Rights, and Women: The Proletarianization of Families in the Late Eighteenth and Early Nineteenth Centuries," *Journal of Economic History* 50 (1990): 17–42; and D. Levine, "Proto-Industrialization and Demographic Upheaval," in L. P. Moch, ed., *Essays on the Family and Historical Change* (College Station, TX: Texas A&M University Press, 1983), 9–34.

79. Benenson, "The 'Family Wage' and Working Women's Consciousness in Britain," 71–101; and Barrett and McIntosh, "The 'Family Wage': Some Problems for Socialists and Feminists," 51–72.

80. Anna Martin, *The Mother and Social Reform* (London: NUWSS, 1895), 60–61; and J. Lewis, *Women in England*, 51–52.

81. Horrell and Humphries, "Class Struggle and the Persistence of the Working Class Family," 248.

82. Jane Humphries, "The Working Class Family: A Marxist Perspective," in Jean Bethke Elshtain, ed., *The Family in Political Thought* (Amherst, MA: University of Massachusetts Press, 1982), 217.

83. Cornell and Karlsson, "Arbetets Sociala form," 393–415.

84. Lisa Peattie and Martin Rein, *Women's Claims: A Study in Political Economy* (Oxford: Oxford University Press, 1983).

85. Horrell and Humphries, "Class Struggle and the Persistence of the Working Class Family," 247.

86. Reuben Gronau, "Home Production: A Forgotten Industry," *Review of Economics and Statistics* 62 (1980): 408–16.

87. Ibid.

88. Scott Burns, *The Household Economy: Its Shape, Origin, and Future* (Boston: Beacon Press, 1989), 23.

3. Alexander Chayanov and the Theory of Peasant Utopia

1. That George Orwell would choose the same year for the title of his 1947 dystopian novel is possibly no coincidence. It is fairly certain that both Chay-

anov and Orwell borrowed this iconic future date from a 1907 work by Jack London titled *The Iron Heel.* It is also possible that Chayanov's visit to England in 1922, and his conversations with English associates about his utopia, created an "oral tradition" that would later "remind Orwell of a date he had read, but perhaps not consciously noted, in *The Iron Heel.*" See R. E. F. Smith, "Notes on the Sources of George Orwell's *1984*," *Journal of Peasant Studies* 4 (Oct. 1976): 9–10.

2. Ivan Kremnev (pseudonym of A. V. Chayanov), "The Journey of My Brother Alexei to the Land of Peasant Utopia," *Journal of Peasant Studies* 4 (Oct. 1976): 75, 77, 79, 83.

3. R. E. F. Smith, "Introduction," *Journal of Peasant Studies* 4 (Oct. 1976): 5.

4. P. Orlovskii, "Forward," "The Journey of My Brother Alexei," 65–70.

5. Kremnev, "The Journey of My Brother Alexei," 83.

6. Ibid., 89–90.

7. Ibid., 84, 88.

8. Ibid.

9. Ibid., 90–91.

10. Ibid., 97–99, 112.

11. Ibid., 97–99.

12. Ibid., 114–15.

13. A phrase applied to Chayanov in: Marc Edelman, "Bringing the Moral Economy Back in . . . the Study of 21st Century Transnational Peasant Movements," *American Anthropologist* 107 (no. 3, 2005): 331–33.

14. See: Mark Harrison, "Chayanov and the Economics of the Russian Peasantry," *Journal of Peasant Studies* 2 (July 1975): 389; F. Sanchez de Puerta, "Chayanov and Social Agronomy in Russia (1918)," at http://library.wur.nl/ejae/vln 3–2.html (12/6/2006): 2; and Daniel Thorner, "Chayanov's Concept of Peasant Economy," in A. V. Chayanov, *The Theory of Peasant Economy* (Madison, WI: University of Wisconsin Press, 1986), xii.

15. A. V. Chayanov, *Peasant Farm Organization* (Moscow: The Cooperative Publishing House, 1925), 37–38.

16. Mark Harrison, "The Peasant Mode of Production in the Work of A. V. Chayanov," *Journal of Peasant Studies* 4 (July 1977): 333.

17. Harrison, "Chayanov and the Economics of the Russian Peasantry," 393.

18. Teodor Shanin, *The Awkward Class: Political Sociology of Peasantry in a Developing Society: Russia 1910–1925* (Oxford: Clarendon Press, 1972), 105.

19. Chayanov, *Peasant Farm Organization*, 43.

20. Ibid., 46. See also Edelman, "Bringing the Moral Economy Back in . . . ," 334.

21. Gary Littlejohn, "Peasant Economy and Society," in Barry Hindess, ed., *Sociological Theories of the Economy* (New York: Holmes & Meier, 1977), 121.

22. Noted in Thorner, "Chayanov's Concept of Peasant Economy," xv.

23. A. V. Chayanov, "On the Theory of Non-Capitalist Economic Systems [1924]," in Chayanov, *The Theory of Peasant Economy*, 4, 11; also Chayanov, *Peasant Farm Organization*, 42. Early on, Chayanov posited two other economies as well ("serf" and "feudal"); he decided in the end that these were merely variations of the "family economy." See Thorner, "Chayanov's Concept of Peasant Economy," xxii.

24. Chayanov, "On the Theory of Non-Capitalist Economic Systems," 25, 27.

25. Chayanov, *Peasant Farm Organization*, 48.

26. R. Roberts and T. Mutersbaugh, "Commentary," *Environment and Planning* 28 (1996): 952.

27. Chayanov, *Peasant Farm Organization*, 86.

28. Ibid., 4.

29. Chayanov, "On the Theory of Non-Capitalist Economic Systems," 5.

30. Harrison, "The Peasant Mode of Production in the Work of A. V. Chayanov," 332.

31. Teodor Shanin, "Chayanov's Message: Illuminations, Miscomprehensions, and the Contemporary 'Development Theory,'" in Chayanov, *The Theory of Peasant Economy*, 6.

32. Harrison, "The Peasant Mode of Production in the Work of A. V. Chayanov," 324; and Harrison, "Chayanov and the Economies of the Russian Peasantry," 407.

33. Chayanov, *Peasant Farm Organization*, 42.

34. Harrison, "Chayanov and the Economics of the Russian Peasantry," 390.

35. Chayanov, "On a Theory of Non-Capitalist Economic Systems," 24.

36. See: Teodor Shanin, "The Nature and Logic of the Peasant Economy II: Diversity and Change; III: Policy and Intervention," *Journal of Peasant Studies* 1 (Jan. 1974): 201.

37. Thorner, "Chayanov's Concept of Peasant Economy," xx.

38. Chayanov, "On a Theory of Non-Capitalist Economic Systems," 13.

39. Chayanov, *Peasant Farm Organization*, 39–41, 225.

40. Andrew Lytle, "The Hind Tit," in *I'll Take My Stand: The South and the Agrarian Tradition* (Baton Rouge, LA: Louisiana State University Press, 1977 [1930]), 241.

41. Shanin, *The Awkward Class*, 101.

42. Chayanov, *Peasant Farm Organization*, 257.

43. Ibid., 54. Emphasis added.

44. Teodor Shanin, "The Nature and Logic of the Peasant Economy I: A Generalisation," *Journal of Peasant Studies* 1 (Oct. 1973): 68.

45. Thorner, "Chayanov's Concept of Peasant Economy," xvii.

46. Harrison, "The Peasant Mode of Production in the Work of A. V. Chayanov," 330.

47. Chayanov, *Peasant Farm Organization*, 41.

48. Ibid., 64, 94, 101. See also Shanin, "The Nature and Logic of the Peasant Economy I: A Generalization," 70; and Harrison, "The Peasant Mode of Production in the Work of A. V. Chayanov," 333.

49. Chayanov, *Peasant Farm Organization*, 5–7, 92.

50. Ibid., 42.

51. Ibid., 48, 57–63, 69. See also Shanin, *The Awkward Class*, 102; and Harrison, "Chayanov and the Economics of the Russian Peasantry," 398.

52. Chayanov, "On a Theory of Non-Capitalist Economic Systems," 13.

53. Alexander Chayanov, *The Theory of Peasant Co-operatives*, trans. by David Wedgwood Benn (Columbus: Ohio State University Press, 1991 [1927]), 5.

54. Chayanov, *Peasant Farm Organization*, 96; and Roberts and Mutersbaugh, "Commentary," 953–54.

55. Roberts and Mutersbaugh, "Commentary," 954.

56. Thorner, "Chayanov's Concept of Peasant Economy," xvii.

57. Puerta, "Chayanov and Social Agronomy in Russia," 4.

58. Chayanov, *Peasant Farm Organization*, 256.

59. Chayanov, *The Theory of Peasant Co-operatives*, 10. Emphasis added.

60. Ibid., 10–11. Emphasis added.

61. Ibid., 22.

62. Littlejohn, "Peasant Economy and Society," 118.

63. James Scott, *The Moral Economy of the Peasant* (New Haven, CT: Yale University Press, 1976).

64. Edelman, "Bringing the Moral Economy Back in . . . ," 341.

65. Harrison, "The Peasant Mode of Production in the Work of A. V. Chayanov," 331.

4. Green Rising: The Promise and Tragedy of Peasant Rule in Eastern Europe

1. G. K. Chesterton, "Introduction," in Helen Douglas-Irvine, *The Making of Rural Europe* (London: George Allen & Unwin, 1923), 7–8.

2. Douglas-Irvine, *The Making of Rural Europe*, 202.

3. Robert Bideleux and Ian Jeffries, *A History of Eastern Europe: Crisis and Change* (London and New York: Routledge, 1998), 445.

4. Robert Redfield, *Peasant Society and Culture: An Anthropological Approach to Civilization* (Chicago: University of Chicago Press, 1956), 31.

5. H. Hessell Tiltman, *Peasant Europe* (London: Jarrolds, 1936), 14–16, 18–19, 25.

6. David Mitrany, *The Land and the Peasant in Rumania* (London: Oxford University Press, 1930), 104.

7. David Mitrany, *Marx Against the Peasant: A Study in Social Dogmatism* (London: George Weidenfeld and Nicolson, 1951), 139; also 117, 140.

8. Tiltman, *Peasant Europe*, 25, 158.

9. Bideleux and Jeffries, *A History of Eastern Europe*, 443.

10. In Henry L. Roberts, *Rumania: Political Problems of an Agrarian State* (New Haven, CT: Yale University Press, 1951), 145.

11. From Mitrany, *Marx Against the Peasant*, 155, 157.

12. Ibid., 151–53, 162.

13. In Roberts, *Rumania*, 163.

14. From George D. Jackson Jr., *Comintern and Peasant in Eastern Europe, 1919–1930* (New York: Columbia University Press 1966), 43.

15. John D. Bell, *Peasants in Power: Alexander Stamboliski and the Bulgarian Agrarian National Union, 1899–1923* (Princeton, NJ: Princeton University Press, 1977), 160.

16. Paul Gentizon, *Le Drame bulgare (de Ferdinand de Bulgarie a Stamboulisky)* (Paris, 1924): 136–63.

17. Hugh Seton-Watson, *Eastern Europe Between the Wars, 1918–1941* (Hamden, CT: Archon Books, 1962), 76, 92, 95–96.

18. Joseph Rothschild, *East Central Europe Between the Two World Wars* (Seattle: University of Washington Press, 1974), 15–16, 18, 328.

19. Jackson, *Comintern and Peasant in Eastern Europe*, 18, 20, 42.

20. Bell, *Peasants in Power*, 155–66.

21. George Dimitrov, "Agrarianism," in Feliks Gross., ed., *European Ideologies: A Survey of 20th Century Political Ideas* (New York: Philosophical Library, 1948), 410–11.

22. Mitrany, *Marx Against the Peasant*, 131.

23. Branko Peselj, *The Industrialization of Peasant Europe* (New York: National Center for a Free Europe, 1953), 12.

24. R. J. Crampton, *Eastern Europe in the Twentieth Century* (London and New York: Routledge, 1994), 153.

25. In Jackson, *Comintern and Peasant in Eastern Europe*, 8.

26. On this effort, see ibid., 51–73.

27. Bell, *Peasants in Power*, 59, 71.

28. Dimitrov, "Agrarianism," 397–400, 416.

29. Irwin Sanders, "Characteristics of Peasant Societies," in Edmund de S. Brunner, Irwin T. Sanders, and Douglas Ensminger, eds., *Farmers of the World: The Development of Agricultural Extension* (New York: Columbia University Press, 1945), 38–39; and Clayton Whipple, "Extension in the Balkans," *Farmers of the World*, 104.

30. Peselj, *The Industrialization of Peasant Europe*, 14.

31. Mitrany, *The Land and the Peasant in Romania*, 496.

32. Bell, *Peasants in Power*, 71.

33. "Peasant Program," adopted in London, July 9, 1942; in Feliks Gross, ed. *Crossroads of Two Continents: A Democratic Federation of East-Central Europe* (New York: Columbia University Press, 1945), 113.

34. In Bell, *Peasants in Power*, 162. Bell notes that John Locke held a similar view of the right to property. Writing in his *Treatise on Civil Government*, Locke stated: "As much land as a man tills, plants, improves, cultivates, and can use the product of, so much is his property." See *Peasants in Power*, 163.

35. Mitrany, *Marx Against the Peasant*, 129.

36. Dimitrov, "Agrarianism," 414.

37. Ibid., 411.

38. Bell, *Peasants in Power*, 163, 167.

39. Ibid., 412, 422.

40. Peselj, *The Industrialization of Peasant Europe*, 18, 32.

41. "Peasant Program," 115.

42. Mitrany, *Marx Against the Peasant*, 125.

43. Tiltman, *Peasant Europe*, 265, 269.

44. In Roberts, *Rumania*, 151.

45. Ibid., 160.

46. Ibid., 146. Emphasis added.

47. "Peasant Program," 113.

48. In Roberts, *Rumania*, 151.

49. Bell, *Peasants in Power*, 169.

50. Ibid., 168.

51. Dimitrov, "Agrarianism," 423.

52. "Peasant Program," 114.

53. Peselj, *The Industrialization of Peasant Europe*, 17.

54. Bell, *Peasants in Power*, 62–63, 67.

55. Peselj, *The Industrialization of Peasant Europe*, 11.

56. Dimitrov, "Agrarianism," 406.

57. Ibid., 401–2.

58. Bell, *Peasants in Power*, 59–60, 64, 66.

59. Sanders, "Characteristics of Peasant Societies," 39.

60. Peselj, *The Industrialization of Peasant Europe*, 11.

61. Bell, *Peasants in Power*, 179, 182.

62. Tiltman, *Peasant Europe*, 72. Emphasis in original.

63. Bell, *Peasants in Power*, 176.

64. Brideleux and Jeffries, *A History of Eastern Europe*, 450.

65. In Dimitrov, "Agrarianism," 423.

66. Bell, *Peasants in Power*, 81, 176–78.

67. "Peasant Program," 115–16.

68. Bell, *Peasants in Power*, 171–73.

69. Dimitrov, "Agrarianism," 422.

70. Bell, *Peasants in Power*, 175–76.

71. Tiltman, *Peasant Europe*, 262.

72. Bell, *Peasants in Power*, 85.

73. Jozo Tomasevich, *Peasants, Politics, and Economic Change in Yugoslavia* (Stanford, CA: Stanford University Press, 1955), 256.

74. Sanders, "Characteristics of Peasant Society," 40.

75. Tomasevich, *Peasants, Politics, and Economic Change in Yugoslavia*, 255.

76. In Bell, *Peasants in Power*, 58.

77. Mitrany, *Marx Against the Peasantry*, 159.

78. Dimitrov, "Agrarianism," 425.

79. Mitrany, *Marx Against the Peasant*, 147.

80. Dimitrov, "Agrarianism," 451.

81. Tiltman, *Peasant Europe*, 225–34; Dimitrov, "Agrarianism," 438–39.

82. In Bell, *Peasants in Power*, 228.

83. Ibid., 146–53; 228–41; Crampton, *Eastern Europe in the Twentieth Century*, 119–23; and Dimitrov, "Agrarianism," 425.

84. Dimitrov, "Agrarianism," 440–44; and Mitrany, *Marx Against the Peasant*, 148.

85. See Philip Gabriel Eidelberg, *The Great Rumanian Peasant Revolt of 1907: Origins of a Modern Jacquerie* (Leiden: E. J. Brill, 1974), 205–16.

86. In Mitrany, *The Land and the Peasant in Rumania*, 101.

87. In Ibid., 113.

88. Roberts, *Rumania*, 135.

89. In Tomasevich, *Peasants, Politics and Economic Change in Yugoslavia*, 347.

90. Ibid., 254–59; 309–15, 344–53, 411–29; and Dimitrov, "Agrarianism," 427–29.

91. Seton-Watson, *Eastern Europe Between the Wars*, 80.

92. Cited in Bidileux and Jeffries, *A History of Eastern Europe*, 448.

93. Rothschild, *East Central Europe Between the Two World Wars*, 18.

94. Bidileux and Jeffries, *A History of Eastern Europe*, 453.

95. Ibid., 452.

96. Ibid., 456.

97. Mitrany, *Marx Against the Peasant*, 140.

98. Mitrany, *Marx Against the Peasant*, 148.

99. Tiltman, *Peasant Europe*, 73.

5. Last March of the Swedish Socialist Housewives

1. Marquis W. Childs, *Sweden: The Middle Way* (New Haven, CT: Yale University Press, 1974 [1936]), xiv.

2. Childs, *Sweden*, 1–5, 13–15, 20–24.

3. For a classic statement of this view, see Charlotte Perkins Gilman, *Women and Economics: A Study of the Economic Relation between Men and Women as a Factor in Social Evolution* (New York: Harper and Row, 1966 [1898]).

4. Frederick Engels, *The Origin of the Family, Private Property and the State*, trans. Ernest Untermann (Chicago: Charles H. Kerr Company, 1902 [1884]), 89–90, 96.

5. Ibid., 90–91; see also Christina Carlsson, *Kvinnosyn och Kvinnopolitik: En studie av svensk socialdemokrati i 1880–1910* (Lund: Arkiv avhandlings serie 25, 1986), 32–55.

6. See Yvonne Hirdman, *Den socialistiska hemmafrun* (Stockholm: Carlssons, 1992), 46–48.

7. Hirdman, *Den socialistiska hemmafrun*, 39–40.

8. Ellen Key, *The Woman Movement* (New York: G. P. Putnam's Sons, 1912), 170, 211–12.

9. Key, *The Woman Movement*, 170, 175, 215. Emphasis in original.

10. Ibid., 163, 171, 213–14.

11. Ibid., 177, 186–87. Emphasis in original.

12. Ibid., 198–206. Emphasis in original.

13. Ibid., 218–19. Emphasis in original.

14. Hirdman, *Den socialistiska hemmafrum*, 53–57.

15. Ibid., 66–83.

16. Alva Myrdal, "Kollektiv bostadsform," *Tiden* 24 (Dec. 1932): 602.

17. Myrdal, "Kollektiv bostadsform," 607.

18. Alva Myrdal, "Kollektivhuset," *Hertha* (Jan. 1933): 11; and Alva Myrdal, "Yrkeskvinnans barn," *Yrkeskvinnor Klubbnytt* (Feb. 1933): 63.

19. Alva and Gunnar Myrdal, *Kris i befolkningsfrågan* (Stockholm: Bonniers, 1934), 319. More broadly, see Yvonne Hirdman, "Utopia in the Home," *International Journal of Political Economy* 22 (Summer 1992): 27–46; and Allan Carlson, *The Swedish Experiment in Family Politics: The Myrdals and the Interwar Population Crisis* (New Brunswick, NJ: Transaction, 1990), 35–99.

20. Myrdal and Myrdal, *Kris i befolkningsfrågan*, 209. See also Gunnar Myrdal, *Hur styrs landet?* (Stockholm: Raben & Sjogren, 1982), 194.

21. Carlson, *The Swedish Experiment in Family Politics*, 177–84.

22. Gunnar Myrdal to Johan Persson and Disa Västberg, Dec. 15, 1938, *Gunnar Myrdal Arkiv* 11.2.4, Arbetarrörelsens Arkiv, Stockholm, 4.

23. Nils Elvander, "A New Swedish Regime for Collective Bargaining and Conflict Resolution." Paper prepared for the Department of Economics, University of Uppsala, 2002.

24. Johanna Overud, "I Beredskap med Fru Lojal: Husmodern i nationens tjänst 1939–1945," in Helena Bergman and Peter Johansson, eds., *Familje*

angelägenheter: Om välfärdstat, genus och politik (Stockholm: Brutus Östlings Bokförlag Symposion, 2002), 85–99.

25. On the formation of this new commission and its conservative nature, see Ann-Katrin Hatje, *Befolkningsfrågan och välfärden: Debatten om familje-politik och nativitetsökning under 1930-och 1940-talen* (Stockholm: Allmänna förlaget, 1974), 47–85.

26. From Yvonne Hirdman, "'Social Planning Under Rational Control': Social Engineering in Sweden in the 1930's and 1940's," in Pauli Kettanen and Hanna Eskola, *Models, Modernity and the Myrdals* (Helsinki: Renvall Institute for Area and Cultural Studies, University of Helsinki, 1997), 72.

27. Quoted in Hirdman, "Utopia in the Home," 80.

28. Statens Offentliga Utrudningen [SOU] 1947: 46, *Betänkande angående Familjliv och Hemarbete* (Stockholm: K.L. Beckman's Boktryckerie, 1947), 157.

29. SOU 1947:46, *Betänkande angående Familjliv och Hemarbete*, 140.

30. Statens Offentliga Utrudningen 1945:4, *Betänkande angående Den Husliga Utbildningen. Angivet av 1941 års Befolkningsutredningen* (Stockholm: K.I. Beckmans Boktryckerie, 1945), 6–7, 26–33, 56–80, 151–55.

31. Hirdman, "Social Planning Under Rational Control," 75.

32. *Arbetarrörelsens efterkrigs program* (Stockholm: Sveriges Socialdemokratiska Arbetarparti, 1944), 25–26.

33. Radiotjänst, *Att vara kvinna: Elva radioprogram kring temat att vara kvinna i dag, 1948–1949* (Stockholm: Radiotjänst, 1949), 12.

34. Hemmafrun, "Husmödrar upp till kamp!" *Morgonbris* 43 (Jan. 1947): 17.

35. Cover, *Morgonbris* 43 (April 1947); and "Under Frihetens Räda Fanor!" *Morgonbris* 43 (May 1947): 8. Emphasis in original.

36. "Tänk på detta!" *Morgonbris* 43 (Nov. 1947): 21.

37. Alva Myrdal and Viola Klein, *Women's Two Roles: Home and Work* (London: Routledge & Kegan Paul, 1956), 125.

38. E. Stina Lyon, "Alva Myrdal and Viola Klein's *Women's Two Roles*: Women Writing About Women's Dilemmas," Discussion paper at the International Conference: Alva Myrdal's Questions to Our Time, Uppsala, Sweden, March 6–8, 2002, 5.

39. Gro Hagemann, "The Housewife Dilemma: Women's Two Roles Revisited," Paper prepared for the International Conference: Alva Myrdal's Questions to Our Time, Uppsala, Sweden, March 6–8, 2002, 2.

40. Ylva Waldemarson, "Att föra kvinnors talan: LO's kvinnoråd 1947–67," in Chrstina Florin, Lena Sommestad, and Ulla Wikander, eds., *Kvinnor mot kvinnor: Om systerskapets svårigheter* (Stockholm: Norstedts, 1999), 90–92.

41. Yvonne Hirdman, *Med kluven tunga: LO och genusordningen* (Stockholm: Atlas, 1998), 77–81.

42. Christina Florin, "Skatten som befriar: Hemmafruar mot yrkeskvinnor i 1960– talets särbeskattningens-debatt," in Florin, Sommestad and Wikander, *Kvinnor mot kvinnor*, 120–21.

43. Alva Myrdal, "Foreword," in *The Changing Roles of Men and Women*, trans. Gunilla and Steven Anderman, ed. Edmund Dahlström (Boston: Beacon Press, 1971 [1962]), 14–15.

44. Nancy Eriksson, *Bara en hemmafru: En debattinlägg om kvinnan i familjen* (Stockholm: Forum, 1964), 36–37.

45. Eriksson, *Bara en hemmafru*, 61–62.

46. Dorothy McBride Stetson and Amy Maxur, eds., *Comparative State Feminisms* (Thousand Oaks, CA: SAGE Publications, 1995), 241.

47. Quoted in Stetson and Mazur, *Comparative State Feminisms*, 241. See also Lilja Mosesdottir, "Pathways Towards the Dual Breadwinner Model: The Role of the Swedish, German, and American States," paper prepared for the Social Sciences Educational and Research Center, Luleå, Sweden, 2000: 15–16.

48. Florin, "Skatten som befriar," 111, 114.

49. Siv Gustafsson, "Separate Taxation and Married Women's Labor Supply: A Comparison of West Germany and Sweden," *Journal of Population Economics* 5 (1992): 63–64.

50. Kerstin Sörensen and Christina Bergquist, *Gender and the Social Democratic Welfare Regime: A Comparsion of Gender-Equality Friendly Policies in Sweden and Norway* (Stockholm: Arbetslivsinstitutet, 2002), 9.

51. Quoted in Jane Lewis and Gertrude Åström, "Equality, Difference, and State Welfare: Labor Market and Family Politics in Sweden," *Feminist Studies* 18 (Spring 1992): 67.

52. Alva Myrdal et al., *Toward Equality: The Alva Myrdal Report to the Swedish Social Democratic Party* (Stockholm: Prisma, 1972 [1969]), 17, 38, 64, 82–84.

53. Florin, "Skatten som befriar," 109–13.

54. Ibid., 126–29.

55. *SAP Congress Minutes*, 1972, 759; quoted in Yvonne Hirdman, "The Importance of Gender in the Swedish Labor Movement: Or a Swedish Dilemma," Paper prepared for the Swedish National Institute of Working Life, 2002: 6.

56. Florin, "Skatten som befriar," 107.

57. An insight borrowed from: Hirdman, "Utopia in the Home," 29.

58. Hirdman, "The Importance of Gender in the Swedish Labor Movement," 10.

6. Karl Polanyi and the "Economy without Markets"

1. Karl Polanyi, *The Great Transformation* (New York: Farrar & Rinehart, 1944), 104.

2. Karl Polanyi, "The Economy as Instituted Process," in Karl Polanyi, Conrad M. Arensberg, and Harry W. Pearson, eds., *Trade and Market in the Early Empires* (New York: The Free Press, 1957), 263.

3. Kari Polanyi-Levitt, ed., *The Life and Work of Karl Polanyi* (Montreal/New York: Black Rose Books, 1990), 78.

4. Quoted in Ibid., 8.

5. Lee Congdon, "The Sovereignty of Society: Polanyi in Vienna," in Polanyi-Levitt, *The Life and Work of Karl Polanyi*, 83.

6. See Bryce Christensen, "Sell Out: Advertising's Assault on the Family," *The Family in America* 4 (Feb. 1990): 2; and Bryce Christensen, "Homeless America—Why Has America Lost Its Homemakers?" Chapter 5 of *Divided We Fall: Family Discord and the Fracturing of America* (New Brunswick, NJ: Transaction Books, 2005).

7. Robert Nisbet, *The Quest for Community: A Study in the Ethics of Order and Freedom* (San Francisco: Institute for Contemporary Studies, 1990 [1953]), 247. Emphasis added.

8. Ibid., 212.

9. Ibid., 214–15.

10. Peter F. Drucker, *Adventures of a Bystander* (New York: Harper & Row, 1978), 138.

11. For a brief intellectual biography of Michael Polanyi, see Mark T. Mitchell, *Michael Polanyi: The Art of Knowing* (Wilmington, DE: ISI Books, 2006).

12. Polanyi, *The Great Transformation,* 3. Emphasis added.

13. Ibid., 72–73.

14. See Fred Block, "Karl Polanyi and the Writing of *The Great Transformation*," *Theory and Society* 32 (2003): 275.

15. Ibid., 44.

16. Ibid., 46.

17. Ibid., 99.

18. Karl Polanyi, "Aristotle Discovers the Economy," in Polanyi et al., *Trade and Markets in the Early Empire*, 69–70.

19. Polanyi, *The Great Transformation*, 111–12.

20. Ibid., 125.

21. Ibid., 98–114, 125, 224.

22. Ibid., 85.

23. Ibid., 123.

24. Ibid., 126.

25. Ibid., 25.

26. Ibid., 40, 138.

27. Ibid., 139–40.

28. On this point, see: Keith Rankin, "Karl Polanyi on the Utopia of the

'Self-Regulating Market,'" at http://keithrankin.co.nz/nzpr1998_4Polanyi. html (3/1/2005): 2.

29. Ibid., 3–6.

30. Drucker, *Adventures of a Bystander*, 140.

31. Polanyi, *The Great Transformation*, 39.

32. See J. Ron Stanfield, "Karl Polanyi and Contemporary Economic Thought," in Polanyi-Levitt, *The Life and Work of Karl Polanyi*, 197–98.

33. Polanyi, "Aristotle Discovers the Economy," 66.

34. Quoted in Stanfield, "Karl Polanyi and Contemporary Economic Thought," 115.

35. Polanyi, "Aristotle Discovers the Economy," 81.

36. See Polanyi et al., *Trade and Market in the Early Empires*, Chapters 2–4, 7–11.

37. Drucker, *Adventures of a Bystander*, 137.

38. Joseph Stiglitz, foreword to the 2001 edition of *The Great Transformation* (Boston: Beacon Press, 2001), vii–vxii.

39. Block, "Karl Polanyi and the Writing of *The Great Transformation*," 275. See also the essays in Kenneth McRobbie and Kari Polanyi-Levitt, eds., *Karl Polanyi in Vienna: The Contemporary Significance of The Great Transformation* (Montreal and New York: Black Rose Books, 2000).

40. On this system, see chapter 2.

7. Seeking a Moral Economy: The Christian Democratic Moment

1. At http://www.buchanan.org/pa-92-0817-rnc.html (7/11/2005).

2. Abraham Kuyper, "Uniformity: The Curse of Modern Life," in James D. Bratt, ed., *Abraham Kuyper: A Centennial Reader* (Grand Rapids, MI: William B. Eerdmans, 1998), 24.

3. Abraham Kuyper, "Maranatha," in Bratt, *Abraham Kuyper*, 210–11. Also Maria Mitchell, "Materialsim and Secularism: CDU Politicians and National Socialism, 1945–1949," *Journal of Modern History* 67 (June 1995): 286.

4. Mitchell, "Materialism and Secularism," 290, fn. 45.

5. Ibid., 290–21, fn. 46.

6. In: Mario Einaudi and Francois Goguel, *Christian Democracy in Italy and France* (Notre Dame, IN: University of Notre Dame Press, 1952), 81–82.

7. Guido Dierickx, "Christian Democracy and Its Ideological Rivals: An Empirical Comparison in the Low Countries," in David Hauley, ed., *Christian Democracy in Europe: A Comparative Perspective* (London: Pinter Publishers, 1994), 24.

8. Dierickx, "Christian Democracy and Its Ideological Rivals," 24.

9. See: Timothy Sherratt, "Christian and Democrat? The Trans-Political Character of Christian Democracy," *Catholic Social Science Review* 9 (2004): 57.

10. Noted in the entry, "Christian Democracy," found in *The Catholic Encyclopedia*, at http://www.newadvent.org/cathen/04708a.htm (6/24/2005): 2.

11. See: Hans Maier, *Revolution and Church: The Early History of Christian Democracy, 1789–1901* (Notre Dame, IN: University of Notre Dame, 1969), 100–121, 147–49.

12. "Wilhelm Emmanuel, Baron von Ketteler," at http:///www.newadvent.org/cathen/08629c.htm (7/11/2005): 1–5.

13. Pope Leo XIII, *Rerum Novarum*; in *Two Basic Social Encyclicals* (Washington, DC: Catholic University of America Press, 1943), 5–11, 15, 55–59.

14. Leo XIII, *Graves De Communi Re* (January 18, 1901); at http://www.ewtn.com/library/encyc/l13grcom.htm (6/24/2005): 2.

15. Kuyper, "Maranatha," 212.

16. Kuyper, "Uniformity," 32.

17. Ibid.

18. Kuyper, "Maranatha," 222.

19. Ibid., 218–19.

20. See Einaudi and Goguel, *Christian Democracy in Italy and France*, 81–82; and R. E. M. Irving, *The Christian Democratic Parties of Western Europe* (London: George Allen & Unwin, 1979), 30–31.

21. R. E. M. Irving, *Christian Democracy in France* (London: George Allen & Unwin, 1973), 53–54, 58.

22. Irving, *The Christian Democratic Parties of Europe*, 31; and Einaudi and Goguel, *Christian Democracy in Italy and France*, 30–31.

23. Noel D. Cary, *The Path to Christian Democracy: German Catholics and the Party System from Windthorst to Adenauer* (Cambridge, MA: Harvard University Press, 1996), 180; and Einaudi and Goguel, *Christian Democracy in France and Italy*, 28–30, 84.

24. Quoted in Irving, *Christian Democracy in France*, 55.

25. Ibid., 60.

26. Ibid., 61–62.

27. See Emiel Lamberts, ed., *Christian Democracy in the European Union, 1945/1995* (Leuven, Belgium: Leuven University Press, 1997), 440.

28. Wilhelm Röpke, *A Humane Economy: The Social Economy of the Free Market* (Wilmington, DE: ISI Books, 1998 [1957; 1960]), 6, 8, 10, 92, 107.

29. Röpke, *A Humane Economy*, xv–xvii, 94, 99.

30. Ibid., 93, 125, 164. Emphasis added.

31. Ibid., 175–77. The one area where Röpke parted company from Christian Democratic doctrine was on population. While granting "respect" to the Roman Catholic position on birth control, he decided that the "human

flood" of numbers that he saw in the early 1950s threatened social order and progress. See 40–44.

32. For a special focus on the German story, see Cary, *The Path to Christian Democracy.*

33. The movement also sprang up in Latin America, with Christian Democracy particularly strong in Chile. In 1964, Eduardo Frei came to power there with a solid Christian Democratic majority and launched an ambitious program of economic and social reform focused on family and small property.

34. On their respective roles, see Allan Carlson, "The Family is the Natural . . . Unit of Society: Evidence From the Social Sciences," Paper presented to the European Regional Dialogue for The Doha International Conference for the Family, Geneva, Switzerland, August 23–25, 2004.

35. Lamberts, *Christian Democracy in the European Union,* 142.

36. See René Cassin, "Historique de la Declaration Universelle de 1948," in *La Pensée et Action* (Paris: F. Lalou, 1972), 108, 115.

37. Lamberts, *Christian Democracy in the European Union,* 143–44.

38. Although occurring later, the Italian Christian Democratic Party—beset by scandals and infighting—disbanded in 1994.

39. See Ronald Inglehart, *The Silent Revolution: Changing Values and Political Styles Among Western Publics* (Princeton, NJ: Princeton University Press, 1977), 216; and Ron Lesthaeghe, "A Century of Demographic and Cultural Change in Western Europe," *Population and Development Review* 9 (Sept. 1983): 29.

40. Lamberts, *Christian Democracy in the European Union,* 445.

41. See: Adrian Karatnycky, "Christian Democracy Resurgent: Raising the Banner of Faith in Eastern Europe," *Foreign Affairs* 77 (Jan./Feb. 1998): 13–18.

Conclusion: Dreams, Realities, Illusions

1. Polanyi, *The Great Transformation,* 197.

2. From Yvonne Hirdman, "The Importance of Gender in the Swedish Labor Movement: Or a Swedish Dilemma." Paper prepared for the Swedish National Institute of Working Life, 2002.

3. See Lee Rainwater and William L. Yancy, eds., *The Moynihan Report and the Politics of Controversy* (Cambridge, MA: MIT Press, 1967).

4. See Donald T. Critchlow, *Phyllis Schlafly and Grassroots Conservatism: A Woman's Crusade* (Princeton, NJ: Princeton University Press, 2005).

5. Stiglitz, foreword to Polanyi, *The Great Transformation* [2001 edition], xv.

6. Ibid., xv.

7. The Doha Development Round are negotiations sponsored by the World Trade Organization inaugurated at a meeting in Doha, Qatar, in 2001. The

goal is to lower trade barriers between nations of varying prosperity. The talks stalled in 2006 over disputes between developed and developing nations.

8. D. Bradley, "Marriage, Family, Property and Inheritance in Swedish Law," *International and Comparative Law Quarterly* 39 (April 1990): 378–81.

9. Michael S. Coffman, *Why Property Rights Matter* (Austin, TX: American Land Foundation, 2002), 18.

10. Spencer Heath MacCallum, "The Case for Land Lease Versus Subdivision: Homeowners' Associations Reconsidered," in David T. Beito, Peter Gordon, and Alexander Tabarrok, eds., *The Voluntary City* (Ann Arbor, MI: University of Michigan Press, 2002), 371–79.

11. Stewart D. Friedman and Jeffrey H. Greenhaus, *Work and Family: Allies or Enemies: What Happens When Business Professionals Confront Life Choices* (Oxford and New York: Oxford University Press, 2000), 3–16.

12. Government Offices of Sweden, "EU Policy" (April 29, 2004); at http://www.sweden.gov.se (11/8/2004).

13. European Commission, "Modernizing and Improving Social Protection in the European Union: Communication from the Commissioner"; and Herbert Krieger, "Family Life in Europe—Results of Recent Surveys on Quality of Life in Europe," Family Paper #8, The European Commission.

14. *Babies and Bosses: Reconciling Work and Family Life (Vol. 4): Canada, Finland, Sweden and the United Kingdom* (Brussels: OECD, 2005).

15. Wendell Berry, *Home Economics* (San Francisco: North Point Press, 1987), 118.

Index

About the Author

Allan C. Carlson, one of the nation's foremost family scholars, is president of the Howard Center for Family, Religion & Society in Rockford, Illinois, and international secretary of the World Congress of Families. His books include *The Natural Family: A Manifesto* and (from ISI Books) *The "American Way": Family and Community in the Shaping of the American Identity.*